Hyper Focus

Harness the Power of ADHD to Stop Procrastinating in your Mid-Twenties

by Isabelle Palmer

Dear Esteemed Reader,

Thank you immensely for choosing this book to join your collection. We imagine that you've already embarked on an exploration of ideas within these pages, and we couldn't be happier about it!

Now, if you find yourself chuckling, pondering, or even debating with the words in front of you, we'd absolutely love to hear about it. If you can spare a few moments to pen down your thoughts in a review, we would be as delighted as a dictionary on a spelling bee!

An Amazon review would be excellent - but hey, we're far from picky. Whether it's a scribble on the back of a grocery list, a tweet, or even a message in a bottle (though that might take a while to reach us), your feedback is gold.

Writing a review might not be as fun as a spontaneous dance-off, but we promise it'll bring grins to our faces, warmth to our hearts, and incredibly valuable insights to future readers.

With Gratitude,

Bo Bennett, PhD
Publisher
Archieboy Holdings, LLC.

Table of Contents

Introduction

Welcome to this enlightenment journey on how to turn your ADHD into a superpower! This book is designed especially for folks in their mid-twenties struggling with ADHD. Here, you'll find a compilation of scientifically-backed information and philosophically profound introductions to practical strategies focused on helping you harness the power of your unique mind. More so, it seeks to combine humor, knowledge, and deep insights into ways you can channel your ADHD-induced energy into constructive paths.

Don't be fooled into thinking ADHD is a hindrance; it is not —it's an advantage in disguise. With it, you're capable of unparalleled levels of focus, often referred to as hyper-focus. This book cannot promise to cure ADHD, nor does it aim to. It emphasizes understanding ADHD, harnessing it, and transforming it into a positive force for heightened productivity. You're about to learn how you can use your ADHD to fuel a higher capacity for accomplishing tasks, overcoming the pitfall of procrastination and entering into states of hyper-focus.

Our approach intertwines the scientific, the philosophical, and the informal to create a tapestry of relatable, accessible information. Using a conversational style, as though we sat across from each other with a cup of coffee, this book imparts knowledge drawn from various disciplines that will inspire you to not just manage ADHD but thrive fully with it. So, get ready to delve into the world you've lived in, but this time, with a much clearer lens, ready to grasp and embrace the power that's ADHD, and use it to fire-up an evolution towards a more productive self.

Understanding the Book

This narrative revolves around understanding ADHD, the power it holds, and leveraging this power to attain productivity in all facets of life. To grasp the content of this guide entirely, one needs to approach it with open-mindedness and a willingness to adapt.

In the forthcoming segments, we venture into understanding ADHD and why procrastination appears more dominant at specific life stages, especially during the mid-twenties. These initial stages form the foundation for comprehending the fundamentals of ADHD, leading to the process of managing the impacts and ultimately reaping the benefits.

The first chapter offers a comprehensive definition of ADHD with a particular emphasis on the symptoms and challenges experienced by individuals in their mid-twenties. While the scope of ADHD is broad, it is essential to focus on this age group because this stage often signifies the onset of adult responsibilities, which can be particularly challenging for individuals affected by ADHD.

Following the definition, the exploration then shifts focus to procrastination, perceived as one of the common challenges faced by people diagnosed with ADHD. A clear understanding of procrastination's nature will set the stage for managing it better. Exploring the link between ADHD and procrastination furthers this understanding.

It's crucial to factor in that ADHD is not all thorns without roses. Subsequent chapters in the book delve into the unique advantages that come with it and how to harness these for personal growth and increased productivity. The book presents a balanced view between the condition's challenges and its perceived benefits.

The book then proceeds to unpack the concept of 'hyper-focus.' This ADHD characteristic offers a potential advantage in terms of increased concentration. Understanding how to tap into the hyper-focus state and utilize this enhanced focus in the right, productive direction forms a substantial part of this guide.

In the sections on mastering hyper-focus, the book breaks down steps to help readers enter the hyper-focus zone effectively. It touches on how one can maintain this state and even multitask while in hyper-focus, backed by tips and hints to improve the focus further.

At this point, it should be clear that overcoming procrastination is intricately linked to the dexterity in mastering hyper-focus. The book attempts to inspire by incorporating success stories of individuals who transitioned from chronic procrastinators to accomplished doers, mainly through the power of hyper-focus.

Having equipped the readers with strategies to boost focus, subsequent sections guide them to apply these principles in daily life, maintaining the hyper-focus state over the long term. Several tips and tricks also accompany these strategies to ensure that the reader has a comprehensive toolkit at their disposal.

The focus then turns to move beyond procrastination, addressing various macro aspects like setting goals, retraining the brain, and the importance of nurturing the mind through healthy nutrition and regular physical exercise.

Ultimately, the book aims to empower its readers to take control of their lives by implementing the strategies of activating hyper-focus and minimizing distractions. The conclusion sums up the key points, providing a concise look ahead towards a productive life even when living with ADHD.

Lastly, the book ends with an appendix that provides additional reading resources on ADHD and hyper-focus. This is to ensure that the reader can continue learning and growing beyond this guide, continually embracing the strength within their ADHD.

Therefore, at the heart of it, this book is a guide, a beacon illuminating the path to productivity for those with ADHD. It champions the idea that our perceptions are what truly limit us in our battles, and by shifting our mindsets, we can all learn to turn our perceived weaknesses into our greatest strengths.

Chapter 1: Definition of ADHD

Before we dive right into the thick of it, it's crucial to lay a solid foundation by defining what ADHD is. Attention-Deficit/Hyperactivity Disorder (ADHD) is a neurodevelopmental disorder, and it's much more than being just disorganized or scatterbrained; it's a pervasive difficulty in self-regulation. What that means for you is that you're dealing with a unique way your brain is wired, causing an ongoing pattern of inattention and/or hyperactivity-impulsivity that often interferes with functioning or development. Now, let me reassure you, this is not your fault. There's no need to blame yourself or carry undue guilt around because of your condition. To put it more philosophically, ADHD is like the jigsaw puzzle piece that doesn't seem to fit in with the others, but once you figure out its correct position, it contributes to creating a beautiful picture. By the time you reach your mid-twenties, it's likely that the symptoms of ADHD can take on the distinct flavor of procrastination - and that's essentially because tasks that require significant cognitive effort tend to sooner or later end up at the bottom of an endless to-do list. Stick with me here, as we delve further into the world of ADHD and get you to move from constant procrastination to productive hyper-focus.

What is ADHD?

ADHD stands for Attention Deficit Hyperactivity Disorder. It's a condition commonly marked by symptoms such as trouble paying attention, impulsive behaviors, and hyperactivity. It's not just about squirmy kids or adults who can't sit still. This biological and neurological condition can manifest uniquely in each person, meaning that not everyone with ADHD experiences the exact same symptoms.

When it comes to ages, ADHD is no respecter of calendars. While it's often diagnosed in childhood, it follows many into adulthood. The hyperactivity aspect might fade over time, but difficulties with impulsivity and focus continue. If you're in your mid-twenties and have just been diagnosed with ADHD, or are starting to think you might have it, know that this is not uncommon.

In the brain of a person with ADHD, certain regions and pathways didn't develop as they should have, or are functioning inefficiently. This causes irregularities in how a person responds to certain stimuli and carries out tasks. But don't rush to lament this. While these brain differences come with challenges, they also bring a host of hidden strengths that we shall explore later.

Time can be a slippery notion for those with ADHD. It doesn't flow with the same rhythm as it does for others - it's either now or not-now. This lack of a sense of time can be frustrating when deadlines approach or when underestimated tasks stretch longer than your attention span. The not-now tends to remain fuzzy until it becomes the pressing now.

ADHD can also be described as an issue of inconsistent attention rather than lack of attention. People with ADHD are often able to concentrate on tasks that interest them, but may struggle to focus on tasks they find dull or mundane. It's like a mental channel-surfing, as if your brain's remote control has a mind of its own.

Impulsivity, another hallmark of ADHD, means acting without considering the consequences. For an adult in their mid-twenties, navigating the world of responsibilities and relationships, this impulsivity can make things complicated. It can impact decisions related to finances, career, and personal life, sometimes causing serious repercussions.

Though the name ADHD implies hyperactivity, not all types of ADHD include noticeable restlessness or hyperactivity. In some cases, particularly in adults, it might be more of an inner sense of restlessness rather than outward hyperactivity. It's like having a Ferrari engine for a brain with bicycle brakes. Yes, sometimes it seems too fast to control. But let's remember, it is still a Ferrari engine.

If the above sounds familiar, you might have what is referred to as inattentive type ADHD (formerly known as ADD). This type manifests as difficulty with attention and concentration but without much hyperactivity. It is often under-diagnosed, as it tends to be less disruptive than the hyperactive or combined types.

The combined type of ADHD is when both inattention and hyperactivity/impulsivity are present. Here, someone might struggle with focusing, completing tasks, and acting without thinking. This can lead to issues at work or school, in relationships, and at home.

You might wonder where these symptoms come from. ADHD is largely a genetic condition passed down through families. Other risk factors may include premature birth, environmental toxins, or a brain injury. Nonetheless, blaming neither genes nor circumstances is productive. It's about understanding the way you function and thriving within that.

We're all familiar with the idea of a 'normal' brain, one that can focus at will, resist impulses, and sit quietly. That's not what an ADHD brain is. People with ADHD are wired differently. But let's get one thing clear - different doesn't mean inferior. In fact, the ADHD brain is pretty dynamic and can harness incredible energy and creativity when understood and directed correctly.

Many living with ADHD see their condition as a hurdle to fulfilling their potential. They do struggle, yes. But with the right strategies, tools, and mindset, they can exceed their own expectations. Here's an interesting twist: With all that distinctive wiring, the ADHD brain is actually remarkably suited for something particularly beneficial – hyper-focus. But we'll dive into that later!

Recognizing ADHD is the all-important first step. When you understand the cause behind certain behavioral patterns, it makes it easier to manage them. With the right technique, tools, and coping mechanisms, you can excel in environments where traditional methods had failed.

So, if you've been banging your head against the wall, wondering why you can't seem to focus when everyone else can, it's not that you're lazy or unintelligent. You might just be part of the tribe of incredible minds with Attention Deficit Hyperactivity Disorder. Embrace your wiring. There is power in your uniqueness.

Unveiling ADHD in Mid Twenties

If you're in your mid-twenties and are just now starting to recognize the symptoms of ADHD in yourself, you're not alone. Many people learn about their diagnosis later in life, long after the typical age when ADHD is often identified during childhood. It's a bit like discovering there's been an invisible elephant in your room all this time – it was always there, but you weren't aware of it. Understanding that you may have ADHD can be both validating, and somewhat terrifying. Yet, it's an important step towards making sense of certain challenges.

One of the interesting things about ADHD is that it can look different in every stage of life, and particularly in the twenties. This chapter will explore how ADHD manifests itself in this formative decade, the sort of effects it can have, and how you can cope. It's like a signpost you've never noticed on a road you've always taken.

You might have had some form of the 'aha' moment when you first stumbled upon the definition of ADHD. It might have resonated deeply with the challenges you've been experiencing. Heck, you could've been scrolling through social media, hunting for memes or watching cat videos, when you accidentally clicked on an article that blew your mind. You might've read it thinking, "Hey, this sounds like me!" Or perhaps it was more like a creeping suspicion, a slow realization that your struggle with procrastination, focus, and motivation isn't simply due to lack of willpower or personality flaws.

The mid-twenties is a unique life stage. We're navigating career paths, pursuing advanced academic degrees, starting families, or simply figuring out the 'adult' in 'adulting'. It's a tricky, transformative time, without the structure that the school system provided. Some people manage these transitions smoothly, but for those with undiagnosed ADHD, they could be tricky. Employment, relationships, and personal care demand consistency, organizational skills, and emotional regulation – all common trouble areas for anyone with ADHD.

So, what exactly happens here? You've probably heard of 'emerging adulthood', a term coined by Jeffrey Arnett. It's this distinct phase that occurs between adolescence and full-fledged adulthood, characterized by identity exploration, instability, self-focus, and a sense of in-between. Think of it as the academic, fancier term for 'quarter-life crisis'. Well, introducing ADHD into the mix adds another layer of complexity to this period.

ADHD filters every experience you've had, even if you don't know it's there. Those issues with task completion aren't due to laziness. That forgetfulness is not negligence. Those extreme emotions don't make you weak. And that brain fog you've been wondering about? It's all connected to ADHD. The challenges from this neurological disorder are amplified without the right strategies and methods to deal with them effectively.

The difference in ADHD symptoms and impacts between childhood and adulthood is, to use a classic analogy, like the difference between a pond and an ocean. The same weather patterns might affect both bodies of water, but an ocean will experience deeper, wider, and more complex effects. Moreover, the challenges from ADHD aren't exactly bullet points on a checklist - they affect your daily life, relationships and even self-perception.

The tricky bit about ADHD is that it can often fly under the radar. It might not impact your academic performance disastrously. You might be a high-functioning student, worker, or parent, but feeling constantly drained, overwhelmed and stressed.

You might experience feelings of shame, guilt, or frustration when you're unable to meet the same standards as your peers. These feelings can lead to a vicious cycle of self-blame, negative thinking, and decreased self-confidence. And if you've made it this far without realizing that you're dealing with ADHD, it's possible that you've chalked up your challenges to personal failings.

Understanding that it's ADHD can help break that cycle. It can shift the narrative from "I'm lazy" to "I have a neurological difference that makes certain tasks more challenging." This doesn't mean that you're off the hook for your responsibilities – it simply means that you're going to need a different set of tools than others might use.

Whether you're recently diagnosed with ADHD, or you're exploring the possibility of it, expect a cocktail of emotions. Relief, for finally having an answer. Apprehension, for the unknown path ahead. Anger, at missed opportunities or prior misunderstanding. And perhaps, hope, for finally knowing how to navigate the world in a way that makes sense to you.

Remember, it's not about 'fixing' who you are. It's about understanding your unique brain wiring and working with it, not against it. It's about redefining what productivity, accomplishment, and success mean to you. And most importantly, it's about realizing that the coping strategies and accommodations you need aren't an admission of defeat or a sign of weakness. They are simply tools to help you thrive with ADHD.

Unveiling your ADHD during your mid-twenties can feel like walking into a surprise party that everyone else knew about. It's scary, overwhelming, and you don't exactly know what to do with the 'surprise' of it all. The important part is that you're here now, armed with a newfound understanding of yourself, ready to rediscover your capabilities, and start your journey to harness the power of your ADHD.

Why Procrastination is More Prevalent in Mid-twenties

The mid-twenties are an exceptional time in one's life - a transitional period where youthful ambition collides with newfound adult responsibilities and expectations. But for those with ADHD, this time of life can also mean something else – a notable increase in procrastination. Why is this scenario quite common in the mid-twenties? Let's dive deep to explore some reasons for this phenomena.

Firstly, those in their mid-twenties, especially those with ADHD, often face a unique set of demands. The push to establish a career, manage finances, or nurture relationships can trigger increased anxiety and stress. These pressures can sometimes be quite overwhelming, resulting in a sort of decision paralysis, leading to procrastination.

The abundance of choices in our modern world can also contribute to procrastination, especially for individuals with ADHD. They often have many interests and navigate multiple activities simultaneously. While their ability to hyper-focus allows them to make significant progress on specific tasks, when they're flooded with multiple competing tasks, choosing where to focus becomes a challenge, leading them to delay action.

Secondly, the brain's executive functions, which help in decision-making, planning, and prioritizing tasks, mature fully during the mid-twenty stage of life. For individuals with ADHD, these "executive functions" tend to develop more slowly, making it even more challenging to navigate the requirements of adulthood and making procrastination more likely.

Another reason behind the increased procrastination during the mid-twenties revolves around the changes in routines. Mid-twenties often mark a significant shift in lifestyle. College routines give way to the professional world's stricter schedules, leading to a disruption in familiar patterns. This disruption can lead to procrastination as these young adults with ADHD find their footing in these new routines.

Increased independence during the mid-twenties can also inadvertently enhance procrastination. With independence comes increased responsibility, and for adults with ADHD, this responsibility can prove to be overwhelming, leading to denial and procrastination.

Further exacerbating this, the lack of immediate behavioral consequences in adulthood can lead to procrastination. High school teachers and parents often provide constant reminders, but in adulthood, you're on your own. Sometimes the lack of immediate feedback makes procrastination seem like an acceptable strategy for coping with overwhelming tasks.

Even perfectionism, which is quite common in individuals with ADHD, can contribute to procrastination. Striving for the perfect outcome can lead these individuals to delay starting a task due to the fear of failure or making a mistake. It's important to remember that it's okay not to be perfect and progress matters more than perfection.

Moreover, self-esteem issues often come to a head during the mid-twenties, and for those with ADHD, these issues can be magnified. An increased awareness of their ADHD's impact on their life and a perceived lack of success compared to peers can often lead these adults to delay tasks, putting them off for "better days."

Lastly, individuals who have ADHD often possess a remarkable trait where they thrive in spur-of-the-moment pressure. They tend to wait until the last minute to start tasks because the increased adrenaline helps them focus better. While it can sometimes be beneficial, more often, it results in chronic procrastination.

Understanding these reasons behind increased procrastination can help in devising strategies to overcome it. There is no one-size-fits-all solution to overcoming procrastination, as ADHD manifests differently in each individual. Therefore, discovering what works for you is crucial.

Moreover, it's important to realize that ADHD is not a barrier to a successful life. Yes, it can make traditional routes more challenging, but it also brings unique advantages along. People with ADHD are frequently creative, passionate, and possess excellent problem-solving skills. These traits, when utilized appropriately, can lead to remarkable accomplishments.

Considering all these reasons, individuals in their mid-twenties with ADHD may be facing increased levels of procrastination. Still, it's essential to remember that this is just a part of their journey. With the right tools, support, and understanding of their unique traits, they can turn these challenges into strengths, creating a life filled with productivity and gratification.

In the next chapter, we will dive deeper into understanding procrastination, its connection with ADHD, and how to overcome it. By understanding the connection between these two, you can devise better strategies to manage your ADHD and become a productivity master, no matter what stage of life you are in.

Laying this foundation of understanding is the first step for you to harness your ADHD to your advantage and challenge the traditional negative stigma surrounding ADHD. So let's head into the next chapter where we'll explore these connections further and start this amazing journey of self-discovery.

Chapter 2: The Challenge of Procrastination

Procrastination, we're all familiar with it. That pesky little voice in our mind that says, "I'll do it later," is quite a frequent visitor to those with ADHD. Just as we've established ADHD's essence in Chapter 1, this chapter presents an in-depth view of procrastination as it relates to ADHD, framing it as a significant challenge faced primarily during the mid-twenties. As young adults with ADHD, we often feel the pinch to perform in multiple realms of life - academia, workplace, relationships, self-growth, heck, even keeping our room organized. Sometimes, we find ourselves standing in the proverbial corner of chaos, unsure of how to proceed with the tasks at hand. This is where procrastination sneaks in. It makes a home within our insecurities, lack of focus, distractibility, and hinders our potential to act efficiently. However, understanding procrastination is the first step in tackling it. So why does it occur? The science behind ADHD associated procrastination isn't just about being lazy or absent-minded; it has more to do with how our brain works. It's the result of an internal struggle between our 'doing brain' and 'thinking brain', with our ADHD often swaying the balance. Digging deeper into this, you'll discover that procrastination isn't as straightforward as it seems and its link to ADHD is far more complicated than a garden-variety delay. We have to face it head-on and probe its roots to truly unshackle ourselves from its grip. But don't stress, because once we uncover and acknowledge these deep-seated issues, they'll become less of hindrances and more like stepping stones to a more productive life.

Understanding Procrastination

Transitioning over from the challenges of procrastination that you'll often face, let's dive in a bit deeper and truly try to understand what procrastination is. Procrastination, in simple terms, is the act of delaying or postponing tasks or actions to a later time. It's the "I'll do it tomorrow" syndrome, when tomorrow becomes an endless cycle.

Oftentimes, those with ADHD find themselves battling procrastination more than the average person. This may leave you questioning, why does this occur more frequently with people who have ADHD? The answer lies in the difficulties we face with executive functioning, time perception, and emotional regulation. These facets of ADHD can inadvertently feed into procrastination.

When tasks seem overwhelming, or when we're unclear about how to even begin, we tend to put them off. This can come down to the struggle with executive functions - skills that help one to plan, prioritize, and initiate tasks. When these skills are impaired, it's easy to get lost in the enormity of the task, leading to avoidance and subsequently, procrastination.

Furthermore, those with ADHD may struggle with time perception, making it challenging to effectively prioritize tasks. It becomes difficult to differentiate between what is urgent and what can be postponed. And so we delay, we push aside, we procrastinate.

Emotions also play a key role in our tendency to procrastinate. Often, tasks that evoke negative emotions such as stress, anxiety or boredom, are shoved aside. In other words, we avoid the discomfort and seek immediate emotional relief. Yet in the long term, this tactic only compounds the negative emotional impact as the task continues to loom.

But here's where it gets interesting. If we delve deeper into the mechanics of procrastination, we find that it serves as a temporary mood fixer, a reprieve from negative feelings, almost like an emotional band-aid. A study in Psychological Science found that procrastinators, during the act of procrastination, experience less stress and more positive mood states. But, this temporary high comes at the long-term cost of emotional havoc, poorer health, missed opportunities, and self-esteem issues.

The key phrase to remember here is "temporary high." Though procrastination might feel like an escape or a respite, it is a fleeting and unsatisfactory solution. The more we give in to this temptation to delay, the more we reinforce a vicious cycle, training our minds to seek quick fixes rather than addressing tasks head-on.

This understanding of procrastination as emotional avoidance or temporary relief is crucial in devising strategies to combat it. Indeed, understanding why we procrastinate yields a lot more clarity about how to stop it. It's like getting to know an acquaintance better; the more you know, the better equipped you are to manage the relationship.

The good news is that while procrastination might be a familiar enemy for those with ADHD, it is not an unbeatable one. Now, acknowledging that there's a struggle with procrastination is the first step in addressing it. Remember, it's okay to admit that you're a procrastinator. It's not a personal flaw or a testament to your capabilities. It's merely a behavior that's become a habit over time. And habits, with conscious effort, can be changed.

Understanding this, we can turn procrastination around to work for us, not against us. By acknowledging that we procrastinate for emotional relief, we can find healthier, more proactive ways to manage our feelings. By realizing that we have trouble with executive functioning, we can seek tools to help prioritize and break down tasks. And by admitting that we find it hard to perceive time accurately, we can install systems that help us manage time more effectively.

Understanding procrastination also involves coming to terms with the fact that we live in a world that's primed for distraction. A world where every ding of the phone, every new email, every pop-up notification adds another layer to our "to-do" pile. This digital noise can be especially challenging for someone with ADHD. But, with awareness, we can find ways to make the world's 'always on' nature work for us. More on that later.

As we delve deeper into the relationship between ADHD and procrastination in the next section, we'll unravel the specific ways in which these seemingly disparate aspects come together. Each of these ties back into our journey of transforming procrastination into productivity, of turning ADHD from an obstacle into a unique advantage. You're on the right path, we're just getting started, and there's much more to learn and discover.

The Link between ADHD and Procrastination

For many people with ADHD, procrastination isn't simply a bad habit; it's a frustrating part of everyday life. Interestingly enough, research suggests that there may be a scientific and psychological link between ADHD and procrastination. Understanding this link can provide insight not only into why procrastination is so prevalent among individuals with

ADHD, but also how it can be managed or even turned into a strength.

Procrastination is often viewed as an issue of time management or a lack of motivation. However, for many individuals with ADHD, it's often a result of something deeper: challenges with executive function. Executive functions are neurologically-based skills involving mental control and self-regulation. They include things like task initiation, planning, organization, and time management—all areas where many individuals with ADHD struggle.

In other words, what looks like procrastination from the outside actually may be rooted in the struggles with focus, foresight, and impulsivity that go hand-in-hand with ADHD. It might not be that you don't want to start that project or finish that report—it could be that executive function deficits are making it more difficult to get going.

The mental processes involved in planning, starting, and finishing tasks require a level of sustained focus that can be particularly challenging for those with ADHD. Many people with ADHD have a hard time focusing on activities unless they find them highly stimulating or interesting. The challenge of starting tasks that don't spark immediate interest or excitement can often translate into procrastination.

Scientists have found that the frontal lobe, the part of the brain that helps control executive functionality, often works differently in people with ADHD. This means that tasks that might seem simple to others—like starting a homework assignment or beginning a project— can prove to be significant hurdles. This doesn't mean they're insurmountable, though; understanding the neuroscientific reasons behind these challenges can be the first step towards finding strategies to overcome them.

There's also a psychological component to consider. Many individuals with ADHD have spent their lives being told to "try harder," "focus," or "just get it done," despite feeling that they're already trying as hard as they can. This can lead to feelings of inadequacy and failure which, in turn, may reinforce the cycle of procrastination. If you constantly feel like you're failing no matter how hard you try, it's all too easy to fall into a pattern of avoiding tasks and activities in order to avoid that sense of failure.

On top of this, people with ADHD often struggle with time blindness or time insensitivity. This means they frequently underestimate how much time a task will take or struggle to organize their time effectively. When the completion time of a task seems uncertain or overwhelming, it can lead to further procrastination.

ADHD-related impulsivity also plays a role here. People with ADHD can feel a strong impulsivity towards doing what's immediately gratifying. Taking a break to watch a show or play a video game can be far more appealing than starting a mundane task—resulting in procrastination.

The combination of executive function challenges, a history of feeling like a failure, time insensitivity, and impulsivity can form a perfect storm of procrastination. It's important to realize, however, that these obstacles aren't impassable. With understanding, self-compassion, and the right tools and techniques, they can be addressed head-on.

Instead of feeling guilty for procrastinating or beating yourself up for not completing tasks on time, it's crucial to understand the true reasons behind it. Remember, ADHD is not a weakness or a personal failing; it's a different way of processing information and managing tasks. Understanding the link between ADHD and procrastination isn't about finding excuses—it's about seeking understanding, cultivating empathy for oneself, and using this knowledge to develop strategies that work.

The good news is, once that link is understood, you can start turning the tide. It's possible to leverage the unique aspects of an ADHD brain to combat procrastination and be productive. That's where the concept of hyper-focus comes into play—a state of intense concentration that many folks with ADHD are uniquely capable of. Used correctly, hyper-focus can be a powerful tool to break procrastination patterns and turn ADHD into a strength.

Shifting your mindset is key in this endeavor. Recognizing your unique strengths and abilities can aid in converting perceived limitations into opportunities for growth. As we move onto the next chapter, we'll be looking at the potential benefits of ADHD and exploring how it can possibly be leveraged to be incredibly advantageous.

Chapter 3: The Power of ADHD

After dissecting the link between ADHD and procrastination in the last chapter, it's time to flip the script and delve into the strengths associated with ADHD. Yes, you read that right - strengths. This chapter is all about reprogramming the way you view your ADHD, from perceiving it as a burdensome disorder, to recognizing it as a source of unique abilities. As surprising as it may sound, individuals with ADHD possess certain traits that can actually give them an edge in various life arenas. Terms we're used to hearing, like 'restlessness' or 'inattentiveness', mask underlying qualities like high energy levels and universal thinking, qualities that, if harnessed correctly, can be leveraged to your advantage. Imagine being able to channel that energy into highly productive endeavors or learning to navigate your dynamic thought processes to solve problems more creatively. Additionally, the inherent drive for stimulation and novelty that is part and parcel of ADHD can translate to increased resilience and flexibility in the face of change or stress. But how do we harness these powerful attributes? Well, learning to understand and control the pivotal feature of hyperfocus (which we'll explore in the next chapter) will be key. This might seem a tad intimidating, but remember, every individual has a unique set of strengths and weaknesses - ADHD just means your set is a little more distinctive. It's about learning to dance with the rhythm, not against it.

The Pros of Having ADHD

First, it's important to remember that having ADHD isn't really something you can choose to move in and out of, it's an integral part of who you are. Instead of seeing this condition as a hindrance, why not think of it as a unique ability with its own set of advantages? After all, some of our widely celebrated experts in various fields have ADHD. Let's discuss how this condition isn't all thorns, but comes with its own set of roses.

One of the key advantages of ADHD is the ability to think out of the box. Typically, folks with ADHD tend to connect dots that most people wouldn't think to connect, resulting in unique and creative solutions. This capability can be a significant asset in any career field, but particularly those where innovation and adaptability are important.

Then there's the concept of strengths-based living. It's a philosophy that says to focus on capitalizing on your strengths, rather than wasting energy trying to remedy weaknesses. People with ADHD tend to have a unique combination of strengths, including resilience, hyper-focus, and the capacity for intense bursts of productive energy. With the right strategies, these traits can be harnessed and turned into positive, career-boosting attributes.

Hyperfocus, a trait seen among people with ADHD, can be quite advantageous. When you're incredibly interested in a subject or task, your focus can become laser-sharp, allowing you to rapidly absorb vast amounts of information or make rapid progress on a project. The key here is to find ways to tap into that focus more effectively.

There's also the resilience factor, which can't go unnoticed. People with ADHD often have significant experience with overcoming adversity and coping with challenges because living with ADHD often means learning to overcome roadblocks. That resilience translates into an ability to persevere, even when the going gets tough.

For people with ADHD, the world can be experienced in a way that's rich, vibrant, and intense. The use of the five senses tends to be heightened. This can lead to a greater appreciation of details, color, flavor, or melodies. The ability to experience the world in such a vibrant way can contribute to stellar performance in visually rigorous careers, like graphic design or arts.

Another perk of ADHD is the possibility to have multiple streams of thought running concurrently. There's a certain thrill in being able to quickly shift your attention from one idea to another, maintain several ideas in your mind, and seek patterns and relationships between seemingly unrelated concepts. This trait aids in problem-solving and understanding complex systems.

If you have ADHD, you're likely no stranger to spontaneity. While this trait can sometimes be challenging in more structured environments, it can also open up unique opportunities. The ability to notice and adapt quickly to evolving circumstances can be a highly valuable trait in a rapidly changing world.

A person with ADHD often has an entrepreneurial mindset. This is typically characterized by visionary thinking, innovation, risk-taking, and the drive to create and adapt. Many successful entrepreneurs attribute their success to their ADHD, as it enabled them to think differently, take risks, and resist conformity.

And let's not forget energy. Individuals with ADHD often possess a surplus of energy that can be channeled positively into various ventures such as sports, climbing the corporate ladder, or essentially any field demanding a high-energy input.

ADHD can also gift you a different perspective of time. This comes with its challenges, such as occasional problems with tardiness, but can also mean that you're able to work quickly and effectively under pressure. You might actually thrive with last-minute pressure!

Individuals with ADHD have extraordinary empathy and understanding. They frequently excel at reading non-verbal cues and effortlessly bond with others. This heightened emotional sensitivity can be a powerful tool in fields where understanding and relating to others is key.

High sensitivity to the environment, often found in people with ADHD, means that you may notice more, feel more, and experience life more profoundly. That sensitivity can drive innovative thinking and creative problem solving.

Finally, ADHD can spur a deep-seated passion and enthusiasm for things that truly spark your interest. Yes, it might be hard to concentrate on mundane tasks, but when something catches your attention and engages your brain, your dedication and enthusiasm can be unmatched.

In conclusion, having ADHD is much more than struggling with hyperactivity, impulsiveness, and inattention. As we've seen, it comes with an array of unique strengths. Remember, it's not about eradicating or suppressing your ADHD, but rather learning how to harness its power and use it to your advantage in productive ways.

Using ADHD to your Advantage

The cool thing about ADHD is that it's not all bad. In fact, there's a powerful upside if you know how to tap into it. You have the potential to turn your ADHD into a superpower, a tool that opens doors previously unimagined. The key lies in recognizing and leveraging your unique attributes. Unconventional? Maybe. But people with ADHD are rarely conventional thinkers, and that's exactly what makes us so valuable.

See, ADHD isn't like wearing blinders; it's more like using a different kind of lens. You view the world in a unique way that enables you to zero in on specifics amidst chaos. You're often passionate, creative, and intuitive. Your divergent thinking and your ability to hyper-focus can give you an edge in situations where others might struggle to keep up.

Okay, let's dig a bit deeper. ADHD brains are typically wired to respond to what excites or interests us. This behavior has often been labeled as impulsivity or lack of discipline. But what if we reframe this trait? When something intrigues you, your brain shifts into overdrive, and you enter a state of hyper-focus. You become laser-like in your concentration, barrel through tasks, and yield high-quality results.

That's the beauty of this superpower. Let's call it 'Passion-Powered Focus.' When you're thoroughly engrossed in an activity or topic you're passionate about, your ADHD brain channels your energy into that focus. The distractions fade into the background, and you're able to accomplish more.

This isn't to say that everything will always fall neatly into your areas of passion. But here's where you can use intersecting interests. Let's say you're a tech-geek, but your job involves writing marketing copy for a retail brand. You might not be all that interested in women's fashion, for instance, but what if you shift your focus and look at the technology behind the eCommerce platform? Suddenly, there's an intersection where your passion meets your responsibility. See what we did there?

Of course, this doesn't mean you should ignore responsibilities that don't interest you or are not in your areas of passion – that's not a practical way to live. However, this technique can serve as a bridge when your tasks don't naturally align with your points of enthusiasm.

Now let's talk about your creativity, another ace up your sleeve. People with ADHD are often out-of-the-box thinkers. You're able to think in nonlinear patterns and make intuitive leaps that others don't. This makes you a valuable asset in brainstorming sessions, problem-solving, and in positions where forward thinking is treasured.

The key lies in giving your creativity the right outlets and not squelching it because it may seem weird or different. Let your mind wander, jot down your thoughts or draw them out. You never know when that scribble on a napkin could become the next "Eureka!" moment.

Your energy levels, often seen as hyperactivity, can be a great asset too. Yes, channeling that energy fruitfully can be a challenge, but once harnessed, it can prove to be a powerful force. You could be the dynamo that drives a project forward or the spark that ignites a team's enthusiasm.

Moving forward, it's vital to shift your perspective. Instead of seeing your ADHD as a burden, start thinking of it as a unique form of brain wiring that bears gifts. Encourage yourself to think differently, to appreciate your way of perceiving the world. It's not about fitting in; it's about finding your own groove and exploiting it to its fullest.

At the end of the day, harnessing your ADHD as a strength is about amplifying your innate abilities—hyper-focus, creativity, energy—and learning how to manipulate them to work for you. It's about acknowledging your weak spots, of course, but more importantly, it's about recognizing and celebrating your strong points.

So, remember. People with ADHD are not broken or flawed. You are not less. You're just different, and that difference can be a serious advantage if you know how to use it. Embrace your uniqueness, and turn those supposed weaknesses into your greatest strengths.

It's time. Time to step into your power. Time to unlock your full potential. Time to use your ADHD to its full advantage. You've got this.

Chapter 4: Introduction to Hyperfocus

Just as we've established that ADHD isn't a deficiency, but rather a different wiring of the brain that can be harnessed for productivity, it's crucial we introduce a core element of this mechanism: Hyperfocus. Hyperfocus, to put simply, is an intense form of concentration often experienced by those with ADHD. Unlike typical concentration, which can be akin to a small, steady flame, hyperfocus is more like a roaring bonfire—one that consumes everything in its path and makes it easy to become deeply immersed in a task, often to the exclusion of all else. But don't mistake it as a villain; though it has its quirks and tangles, when leveraged correctly, it can be your secret weapon. Imagine those projects you've kept on the back-burner, those mental hurdles you've struggled to jump—through the lens of hyperfocus, they may come within reach. Now, it's not simple as flicking a switch. The intricacies of hyperfocus lie not in triggering it, but rather in channeling it towards productive goals, which we'll unfold in the coming chapters. For individuals with ADHD, learning to direct this intense focus correctly can completely transform their productivity game.

What is Hyper-focus?

Commonly addressed among ADHD circles, hyper-focus is kind of a superpower for those with the condition. If you've ever been so engrossed in a task or project that everything else falls away—like you're in a zone or bubble—that's hyper-focus. It's a state of intense, unwavering concentration where the mind becomes completely absorbed in a single activity or task.

The hinges of the world outside your pursuit may rust and fall off, but the task at hand takes on a level of priority that swathes other ideas in relative obscurity. You could say it's like getting tunnel vision without the detriment usually associated with such a state.

Feeling drawn into your work, becoming one with the task, losing track of time—these are all hallmarks of this state. Now, it's not an 'off and on' switch that you can push at will, but once you tap into this well of focus, your productivity skyrockets.

Hyper-focus isn't just about spending a large chunk of time on a task, though. It's also about the intensity with which you engage in that activity. How deeply are you diving into the task? How completely are you immersing yourself in it?

A good sign that you might be experiencing hyper-focus is that you may feel surprised when you do look up to take stock of the time and notice that much more of it has passed than you expected. Sometimes, several hours may have disappeared, while to you, it may have felt like mere minutes. It's a little like getting lost in a good book and suddenly realizing it's three in the morning.

Now, it's worth mentioning that everyone has the capacity for hyper-focus, not just those with ADHD. It's a zone, a place in your mind that you can mentally 'step into', regardless of whether or not you have ADHD. The difference is, with ADHD, it becomes both a superpower and, sometimes, a weakness.

Why a 'weakness', you might ask? Well, this intense concentration can be so powerful that pulling away can be akin to a physical struggle. It can be incredibly challenging to transition from one task to another or to juggle multiple tasks at once. This rigidity, while useful in certain contexts, can make it difficult to maintain balance in others.

The good news is, by understanding how hyper-focus works and learning to manage this highly intense attention tunnel, you can take control of its power and make it work for you, not against you. Because while hyper-focus can monopolize your time, it can also make you highly efficient and productive if harnessed correctly.

However, remember that hyper-focus is not a 'quick fix' solution. Like any other mental or psychological state, it takes time and practice to master. It's not as simple as telling your brain to 'get hyper-focused', but with the right techniques and strategies, you can learn to tap into and control this high-powered state of mind.

There's also a point to note here that hyper-focus isn't limited to work-related activities. Quite often, individuals with ADHD find themselves in a state of hyper-focus when engaged in their hobbies or activities they find particularly stimulating or intriguing.

Recognizing when you are in this zone, understanding the triggers that lead you there, and leveraging these insights towards your duties — these steps assist in harnessing the power of hyper-focus and turning ADHD into a constructive force. It takes a bit of reflection and practice, sure, but once mastered, it can be a game-changer.

In short, the state of hyper-focus brings about a profound sense of depth and dedication to a singular task. It's the fortress of concentration, erected in the wake of ADHD, that shields distractions and allows profound productivity within its walls. But like any fortification, there are rules needed to maintain balance and security — a topic you'll delve into in the following chapters.

Let this be your introduction to the superpower within you, one you might not have even known existed. With hyper-focus, you can spin ADHD on its head and use it as a tool for productivity, and ultimately, for your success.

The Difference between Regular Focus and Hyper-focus

As we've discussed, focus is a critical aspect of productivity. However, when it comes to ADHD, the concept of focus takes on a new dimension: hyper-focus. It's not just intensified attention; it's a completely different beast. Understanding how it differs from regular focus helps utilize this unique gift of ADHD.

Under average circumstances, focus is described as one's ability to pay attention to a particular task or stimuli while ignoring extraneous details. A well-adjusted focus allows you to finish a book, have an engaging conversation, or even complete your work effectively. While this ability varies among individuals, the consensus is that the regular focus is necessary, and it generally follows a well-adjusted, predictable path.

Many people can switch their focus with relative ease—dipping in and out of tasks without being 'locked in.' It's like carefully steering a bike, gently maneuvering around obstacles, and knowing when to speed up or slow down based on the path ahead.

However, for ADHD brains, the ride is more like an exhilarating roller coaster. This, in essence, is hyper-focus—intense, unswerving attention that can be wondrously productive but equally challenging to pull away from. It's like being strapped into that roller coaster, plunging into tasks with a thrilling intensity, but finding it extremely difficult to get off, even when the ride's over.

Contrary to the general ADHD belief of being 'attention deficit,' hyper-focus demonstrates an extraordinary capacity for undivided attention. Some people with ADHD may entirely immerse themselves in an activity that stimulates them, to the point that they may lose track of time, ignore their physical needs, or fail to recognize other demands for their attention.

A key difference here is control. Regular focus tends to be more controllable—you can decide when and where to give your attention. In contrast, hyper-focus is a state that is harder to master. It's like being swept away by a category five hurricane. You don't dictate the strength, speed, or direction; you are simply caught up.

But don't demean hyper-focus just because you may feel like you lack control at times. This element of ADHD can also lead to significant accomplishments. The same intensity that makes it hard to switch tasks can result in immense innovation, creativity, and productivity. When harnessed, hyper-focus becomes a superpower, letting brilliance and efficiency shine through.

Another difference lies in task selection. A person with a regular focus might find it easier to concentrate on tasks that are essential but potentially dull. Conversely, those with ADHD may struggle with this, finding their hyper-focus kicks in when engaged in tasks that are intensely interesting—to them! It's rather like being selectively passionate or selectively diligent.

Additionally, the quality of the attention also differs significantly. Regular focus tends to be linear, moving systematically from point A to point B. On the other hand, hyper-focus has a 3D characteristic, bringing in an immersive, in-depth perspective. This makes it effective for problem-solving and innovation, where seeing things differently can be beneficial.

The level of energy in both types of focus is noticeably different. Regular focus carries a constant, steady flow of energy, akin to a steady river stream. Hyper-focus, on the other hand, is more like a waterfall—intense, powerful, and profoundly overwhelming, making the experience uniquely engaging.

In conclusion, hyper-focus isn't 'better' or 'worse' than the regular focus—it's just different. Both have their strengths and weaknesses. Recognizing these differences can foster understanding and nurture self-acceptance. We're on the exciting journey of exploring how ADHD can be repositioned from a challenge to an advantage, after all. And when you've got something like hyper-focus up your sleeve, you're already on solid ground.

In the next sections, we'll focus on how to harness hyper-focus, enabling you to tap into that waterfall of potential and channel it productively. So, no matter how intense the ride might get, just remember: you're not being swept away—you're running the river.

How ADHD Enhances Hyper-focus

Continuing from our exploration of the concept of hyper-focus, it's interesting to note a unique facet about ADHD. Now, you may be wondering, how does ADHD enhance hyper-focus? For most people, attention is like a flashlight. It can shine on one thing at a time. But for people with ADHD, that flashlight often operates like a floodlight, illuminating everything around it. This state of heightened focus, as we've learned, is referred to as hyper-focus.

Studies have shown that people with ADHD have the capacity to be intensely focused, so much so that it can be a defining characteristic. This capability leads to undivided attention on a particular interest or activity, leading to hyper-focus. The fascinating part is that ADHD doesn't just enhance focus, it supercharges it. Understand that it's not that you can't focus, you just focus differently. You have a superpower that you weren't aware of until now.

In your mid-twenties, the world is coming at you fast and hard. But with ADHD and the tool of hyper-focus, you have the ability to slow it all down and focus intently on one thing at a time. It's like having a zoom lens that lets you see close-up details that others miss.

Recognizing this monumental shift in perspective is important. You're not broken or damaged just because your brain works differently. You have a strength that countless others don't have. There are plenty of people without ADHD who'd love to have the ability to focus and concentrate the way you can when you're in hyper-focus mode.

But how do you harness this unique strength? That's where a bit of strategy comes in. Here's the trick – it's all about passion. When people with ADHD find something they're genuinely interested in, they can dive into it with unparalleled focus. It's a tunnel vision that's harder to achieve for those without ADHD.

A key aspect of this characteristic is the neurotransmitter dopamine. In brains with ADHD, the dopamine system is often less active. It's this neurotransmitter that lets us mark things as rewarding, and in some folks with ADHD, they need higher levels of stimulation to get the same reward response. Engagement and interest are your tickets to increased dopamine levels which can trigger the hyper-focused state.

The drawback, of course, is that when things aren't stimulating, focusing becomes much harder. It can feel like wading through molasses to try to concentrate on something you're not interested in. This is where the myth that people with ADHD can't concentrate comes from. It's not that they can't focus, it's that they struggle to focus on things they don't find engaging.

This aspect might seem like a roadblock, right? How do you hyper-focus on things you don't find interesting? That's one of the keys we'll dig into in the next chapters. Don't worry, there are strategies you can use to make less interesting tasks more engaging, and that can help you tap into that supercharged focus even when the task at hand isn't inherently stimulating.

The key takeaway here is to understand your ADHD and how it primes you for hyper-focus. Appreciating and acknowledging this unique attribute of your mind can help you to harness this power and become more productive. It does require some patience and practice, though, to figure out what methods work best for you personally.

So, the next time you perceive your ADHD as a disadvantage, remember this: it provides you with a unique capability to engage in hyper-focus, a state of intense concentration that not many can attain. And guess what? You have this power inside of you. You're not a victim of your ADHD, rather, you're someone with a superhuman ability that others could only dream of having.

Throughout the following sections, we'll be exploring the intricacies of managing and channeling your hyper-focus for productivity. We'll decipher strategies for channeling your hyper-focus even when you're required to concentrate on topics that you might not find inherently interesting. The world is an exciting place when you've got the power of hyper-focus at your disposal. It's all about using it to your advantage.

Embrace this aspect of your ADHD. Utilize it to unearth potentials you were previously unaware of. As we move forward, remind yourself that you possess an extraordinary ability and that ADHD enhances this ability, rather than deters it. You're on your way to mastering your ADHD, and therefore, mastering life.

Chapter 5: Mastering Hyper-focus - Part 1

As we take our first steps towards mastering hyper-focus, we're going to start with the basics. You've already gotten a taste of what hyper-focus is and how it can be enhanced by ADHD. Now, let's dive a bit deeper. First off, grasping the mechanics behind entering the hyper-focus zone is crucial. It's not magic or mere luck; it requires certain prerequisites that set the stage for this intensive state of focus. Speaking of setting the stage, your environment plays a pivotal role. Remember, your surroundings can either spur your focus or scatter it. So, arrange a space that minimizes distractions and fuels productivity. Routine and order, too, are power players in this sport — they provide a sense of predictability which propels focus. Now, maintaining this hyper-focused state is the real challenge, and it's not about driving yourself into the ground with endless hours of work. Incorporating breaks and relaxation techniques is key here. Fun fact: your brain keeps problem-solving even when you're on a break. So, don't consider breaks as 'off time'; they just represent a different kind of 'on'.

The Basics of Hyper-focus

Imagine sitting down to start your work, and the next thing you know, hours have passed. But instead of feeling frazzled or exhausted, you feel accomplished, satisfied, and maybe even invigorated. You've just experienced a taste of hyper-focus, a state of intense concentration often associated with ADHD.

So, what exactly is hyper-focus? It's a heightened state of focus that allows you to concentrate on a task or interest for an extended period of time. In this state, you lock onto a task like a laser beam, blocking out everything else, and can accomplish significant amounts of work in a relatively short amount of time.

The science behind hyper-focus is still mostly theoretical, but a few key factors are generally agreed upon. Firstly, it seems to be amplified by dopamine, a neurotransmitter associated with pleasure, reward, and motivation. It's a stronger, deeper form of the everyday focus that most of us experience.

Dopamine levels in the brain influence your motivation and interest in tasks. When you're interested in what you're doing, your brain releases more dopamine, which makes focusing easier. And we're not just talking about a little bit easier - we're talking about the kind of focus that makes time disappear.

However, before you start to rely on hyper-focus as your superpower, remember that with great power comes great responsibility. Hyper-focus, while a powerful tool, can be a double-edged sword. It can make you oblivious to your surroundings, causing you to neglect your basic needs like nutrition and sleep. Also, it might not always kick in when you want it to, such as when faced with tasks you find less appealing or boring.

So, how can you tame this wild, untamed force to work in your favor? The key is to learn to enter the hyper-focus zone intentionally and control it, rather than letting it control you.

Picture the hyper-focus zone as a room where all your essentials for productivity are kept. The key to this room is your interest and mental engagement with the task at hand.

If you genuinely want to achieve or complete the task, the door to the hyper-focus zone becomes easier to unlock.

Understanding the mechanics of entering this zone is one thing, mastering the art is another. Taming this force requires discipline, structure, and a good grasp on your interests and motivations. Finding what motivates you and sparks your interest will lead you naturally to that state of heightened focus. Practice channeling these interests into your tasks, finding the elements that engage you to unlock your ability to hyper-focus.

But remember, it's not just about turning the key and stepping into the room. Maintaining your state of hyper-focus requires a balance. Yes, you'll be able to get loads done, but if you push yourself too hard, you might burn out. It's essential to remember to pace yourself, take breaks, and step back when needed.

To use hyper-focus effectively, a bit of self-care goes a long way. Regular breaks, healthy eating, and consistent sleep patterns will help maintain your psychological stamina, making it easier for you to dip into your hyper-focus state when need be. Plus, it will prevent you from falling into the trap of hyper-focus burnout.

Above all, remember, it's all about balance. Hyper-focus is an extraordinary tool in the ADHD arsenal, but like all tools, it needs to be used wisely. By understanding the core concepts and mechanisms behind hyper-focus, you're setting the foundation to master and control this fascinating mental superpower.

Take the time to get to know your hyper-focus. Explore the boundaries and understand the triggers. Realize what drives you into this state and use that knowledge to your advantage.

Through understanding and practice, you can take this perceived flaw and turn it into your greatest strength. You can learn to harness the full potential of your brain - ADHD, hyper-focus, and all.

Learning to fully harness this tool is an ongoing process. There's always room for growth and adjustment. With the right mind-set, understanding, and strategies, you can tap into this power more frequently, purposefully, and effectively. Let's delve deeper into how you can make that a reality in upcoming sections.

Getting Into the Hyper-focus Zone

The first key to tapping into the state of hyper-focus lies in one major area: your environment. Just like a mechanic needs a well-organized garage to be able to fix a car, you'll need spaces that are conducive to productivity to get into the hyper-focus zone. To make this happen, consider eliminating distractions such as obnoxious noises or clutter. You could also suggest moving to brighter, lighter spaces that generate a positive mood. The goal is to create an environment that stimulates your brain, making it easier for you to tap into your hyper-focus state.

Your environment doesn't have to be perfect though. In fact, one fascinating aspect of ADHD is the way many of us thrive in chaotic environments. Somehow, amidst all the chaos, we're able to hone our focus on a single point and dive deep into it. So, if a cluttered desk or messy office works for you, then by all means, embrace it.

But harnessing hyper-focus goes well Beyond your environment. Consider the role of routine and order in your lifestyle. This might seem like a hassle to some, especially those with ADHD who may struggle with routine, but hear me out. Establishing a routine—even a simple one—can be a powerful tool in the arsenal for the quest towards hyper-focus.

What does a strong routine look like? Simply put, it looks like whatever you need it to. In other words, what matters most is consistency. The routine that will suit you best is one that corresponds to your lifestyle and enhances your productivity. So, try out a few strategies, tweak as you go along, and see what sticks.

Remember that with ADHD, our circadian rhythms can be a wee bit out of tune. Some of us are night owls while others are early birds. That's okay. Embrace it. Set your schedule accordingly and aim to engage in tasks that require higher concentration during your peak hours.

Order and planning are also key. These steps help to build mental patterns that, over time, can lead to increased productivity and improved ability to hyper-focus. By defining what needs to be accomplished, you have a clear path to follow, and this can help you to remain focused and accomplish more.

Try writing down your tasks, breaking them down into manageable steps. This way, not only will you have a clear, organized plan, but you'll also get the satisfaction of crossing items off your list, which can do wonders for motivation.

Time management and prioritization are also critical. With ADHD, it's easy to get side-tracked or lose focus. Avoid distraction by placing reminders around your workspace or by using tools like a timer to stay on track.

Recognize that each time you succeed in staying focused on your task, you are reinforcing that behavior and making it easier to achieve the following time. So don't downplay your small wins; they are a crucial part of the process.

Listen to your body as well. Some people can sustain longer periods of focus, while others need frequent breaks. It's okay to take a short pause every now and then; it can actually rejuvenate you and enable you to maintain high levels of focus when you're back at work.

Don't forget to reward yourself too. If you've managed to remain on task for a specific amount of time, treat yourself. It doesn't have to be anything extravagant. The idea is that giving yourself a reward can help to enhance your motivation and inspire you to continue focusing.

Partial disconnecting can also be helpful. As paradoxical as this might sound, sometimes unplugging from technology can significantly boost your focus. Notifications, emails and other alerts often serve as a distraction and impede your ability to concentrate. So when you really need to get down to business, consider switching off or put your devices on silent mode.

Remember that this is all a process. You're laying out a new track for your brain, and that's not an overnight accomplishment. Be patient with yourself and celebrate small victories. ADHD or not, we're all human, and we all have days when we're just not on it.

Lastly, consider incorporating rest and relaxation techniques like meditation or yoga, which will enable you to achieve tranquility. A calm mind is less prone to distraction and has a greater chance of achieving hyper-focus.

Getting into the hyper-focus zone is possible with the right environment, a consistent routine, appropriate time management, and a willingness to experiment with what works best for you. Even if the journey may seem challenging at first, remember that allowing your ADHD to work for you, rather than against you, is the secret to entering the hyper-focus zone.

Setting Up Your Environment is the first step towards mastering the art of hyper-focus. The essence of your surroundings can significantly impact your ability to concentrate, particularly if you have ADHD. It's like trying to grow a delicate orchid amidst a bustling, noisy city street - the high energy environ will likely prove detrimental. However, in a refined, controlled environment, the same plant can blossom and flourish. Think of your brain as that orchid and your environment as the surrounding cityscape. You can't thrive unless the conditions are just right.

Create A Distraction-Free Space: Having a dedicated, clutter-free zone that allows your mind to roam free can be key. Remember how, in movies, geniuses are depicted in minimalist rooms with nothing but the essentials? It isn't just a Hollywood gimmick. Decoupage, over-stimulated spaces can cause your brain to scatter, inhibiting hyper-focus. Aim for simplicity, with minimal distracting elements. Less is more when it comes to your workspace. A clear desk can pave the way to a clear mind.

Designate Zones: Similar to how you wouldn't sleep in the kitchen or cook in the bedroom, categorizing different areas in your space for specific activities can prove helpful. Establishing these spatial boundaries trains your brain to associate certain spaces with specific tasks, over time, enhancing focus and productivity. So, dedicate a corner of the room for brainstorming, with a comfy chair, a notepad and your favorite pen. Create a different section for task execution, with your computer, necessary files, and a cup of joe by your side. This approach will also make it easier for your brain to transition between 'idea mode' and 'action mode'.

Control The Audibles: Some folks dig silence, while others find a little background noise comforting. Some people even find that light instrumental music enhances focus. It really does come down to personal preference. Experiment with different sounds and discover what vibe helps you zone in. If you're in a noisy setup, noise-cancelling headphones may prove invaluable. Remember though, you're not trying to provide a soundtrack for a movie here; keep it light and unobtrusive.

Bring Nature Indoors: Green spaces aren't merely for parks and outdoor enthusiasts. They can also inject tranquility into your workspace. Various studies have shown the positive impact of the color green and plants on mental health and focus. Intersperse your environment with a bit of greenery – small potted plants, mini succulents, or even a bonsai work. Plus, it's easier on the eyes than a monotonous grey cubicle, and can sprinkle some much-needed positive energy.

The Role of Routine and Order can't be overstated when it comes to mastering hyper-focus, especially for individuals with ADHD. Disorganization can actually work against hyper-focus, serving to distract and interrupt the flow of concentration. A structured environment, on the other hand, can aid in fostering a mental state conducive to sustained and attentive focus. So let's unpack this.

Think of your brain as a vehicle on a race track. It can keep up with the speed and handle the turns impressively well. But, give it an obstacle-strewn track, and it will falter. That's chaos for you. As such, setting up routine and actively maintaining order helps in clearing out your cognitive race track, making hyper-focus more attainable.

So, how exactly do we establish routine? It doesn't have to be complicated. You could start with simple activities like waking up at a set time, making your bed, or having a fixed morning routine. Small habits like these anchor your day and put your brain in a "ready mode." Essentially, they help ease your brain into a focus-friendly state.

What you're aiming for here is to turn these activities into automatic behavior or 'rituals.' And by consistent repetition, your brain starts to predict these activities, priming itself for more attention-demanding tasks. When your brain isn't preoccupied with figuring out what's next, it can fully invest in your selected task—sort of like putting it on a hyper-focus highway. This prediction and preparedness loop also provides a sense of control, a trait that's often lacking in individuals with ADHD.

Project this structure onto larger parts of your day. Have designated times for meals, work, breaks, and other activities. Again, this frees up mental space and reduces decision fatigue. Sure, it might feel like a chore initially, especially if you fancy yourself as spontaneous. But think of it as setting the stage for the rockstar that is hyper-focus.

Now introducing order, and no, it's not the same as routine. We talk about order in terms of the physical environment around you. A cluttered workspace, for instance, can breed mental disarray. You might be stuck with a nagging sensation of something being 'off,' thereby jeopardizing hyper-focus. But an organized workspace eases finding stuff, lending itself to smoother workflow and sustained focus.

It may sound cliché, but "out of sight, out of mind" rings true here. Reduce visual noise, keep only necessary items within your visual periphery, and have a system for organizing your files or projects. Remember, your goal is to minimize disruptions, be it wasting time hunting for that one document or losing your train of thought over a misplaced cup of coffee.

Also, consider using order-enhancing systems like planners and digital tools with reminders or calendars. Not only do these tools bring structure to a chaotic day, but they also serve as external brains, taking over the job of remembering deadlines or tasks. And when your brain isn't preoccupied, you're more likely to achieve that coveted state of hyper-focus.

Establishing routine and order is, in essence, like setting the ideal conditions for hyper-focus to thrive. It's not about stripping away your individuality, but aiding your brain in reaching maximal performance. And once you figure out how to design this structure around your unique lifestyle and preferences, you'll be equipped to better channel the mighty power of your ADHD-fueled hyper-focus.

Maintaining the Hyper-focus State

And now, you're in the hyper-focus state. You've built an environment that supports this enhanced concentration, and you've established a routine that leads you into the hyper-focus zone. But how do you maintain this state for extended periods? How do you ensure that it doesn't become an exhausting roller-coaster ride that eventually crashes?

Fear not, as it's entirely manageable. The trick is, maintaining an effective rhythm between intense focus and relaxation."] Maintaining the hyper-focus state is like surfing. You ride the wave of concentration, but you don't forget to re-energize before the next wave.

First off, let's address why maintaining hyper-focus is essential for people with ADHD. This focused state, when developed and honed properly, allows for managing tasks that may otherwise seem impossible or overwhelming. It provides an opportunity to dive deep into projects and ideas, channeling the innate dynamism of the ADHD mind in a structured, constructive way. And crucially, it offers a defense against the counterproductive allure of procrastination."

Here's where incorporating breaks come into play. It sounds counterintuitive, but scheduling breaks is a scientifically proven strategy for maintaining hyper-focus. Taking a pause isn't idleness; it's a way to ensure your brain can sustain its productivity over time. Its about knowing when to take your foot off the gas and allowing your mental fuel to replenish before hitting the road again.

When in hyper-focus mode, your brain is in overdrive, going a hundred miles an hour. It can be incredibly exhilarating! However, it's also draining if done non-stop. And that's why strategic rest periods are crucial. Contrary to what you might think, giving your mind a rest won't break your concentration. Instead, it'll allow you to redirect your mental resources and return to your work with renewed vigor."

So how long should these breaks be? Research suggests a break of 5-15 minutes after every 50-90 minutes of work, works wonders. These short micro-breaks can help you maintain your hyper-focus state over a longer duration. You would be amazed at how a brief stroll, a nourishing snack, or just taking a moment to breathe can refresh your mind.

But, let's be clear! These aren't invitations to get lost in the labyrinth of social media or the vortex of viral videos. The aim is to take a mental breather, not to introduce distractions that might make it harder for you to enter back into the hyper-focused state.

It's also crucial that you listen to your body. Everyone's rhythm is different. What works for one person might not necessarily work for another. You may find that a 5-minute break every 60 minutes is perfect for you, or you might prefer a longer break every 90 minutes. Experiment and see what rejuvenates you and aids your focus rhythms."

Apart from scheduled breaks, relaxation techniques also play a significant role in maintaining the hyper-focus state. These methods help the mind and the body to recover and reduce stress. Meditation, deep-breathing exercises, yoga, or simply relaxing to soothing music, contribute to mental and emotional health which support a sustained state of hyper-focus."

Becoming aware of your own mindfulness levels is another beneficial strategy. Amidst the rush of a hyper-focused state, it's easy to lose sight of one's emotional and mental state. Regularly checking in with yourself helps you stay in a productive zone without burning out. This reflective practice cultivates a greater self-awareness of your mental capacities, allowing you to recognize when you can push forward and when you need to step back."

Another practical approach involves leveraging the positive aspects of hyper-focus by aligning it with your natural circadian rhythm. Some people do their best work in the early morning, while others peak in the late afternoon or evening. Understanding your natural pattern can help you plan your tasks so that you're working in sync with your body's energy levels, rather than against them.

Finally, it's also about nurturing your body. Proper hydration, a balanced diet rich in nutrients, and regular physical activity will support cognitive functions, including focus. It might not be as flashy as some of the other strategies, but taking care of your physical health is the foundation upon which the hyper-focused state is built."

In summary, maintaining the hyper-focus state involves a balanced combination of intense focus periods, regular breaks, relaxation techniques, mindfulness, syncing with your circadian rhythm, and physical care. By mastering these elements, you can take advantage of the immense potential of your ADHD-derived hyper-focus, transforming it from an unpredictable firecracker into a controlled, sustained energy source that propels your productivity and creativity."

Incorporating Breaks and Relaxation Techniques is an essential step in mastering not only your hyper-focus but also your ADHD. While your unique ability to hyper-focus might give you the power to intensely focus on tasks, it's equally important to give yourself regular breathing spaces. These spaces or breaks act as an important tool to refresh, recharge, and reset your mind, contributing to better productivity and mental well-being.

Now, you might be thinking that taking breaks would cause a disadvantage, especially when you're in a flow state. This is a common misconception when it comes to the art of focus. In reality, cognitive research supports the idea of balancing work sessions with regular intervals of rest. Intense thinking, as done during hyper-focus, exhausts the brain and can lead to mental fatigue. Breaks can aid in preventing this fatigue, promoting sustained attention, and keeping your focus sharp.

Planning your breaks with a system known as the Pomodoro Technique can work wonders. This method advocates 25 minutes of focused work, followed by a five-minute break. After you've completed four 'Pomodoros', you take a longer break of around 15 to 20 minutes. This technique combines the benefits of time-blocking with regular relaxation periods, helping you keep ADHD at bay and capitalize on your propensity to hyper-focus.

Apart from regular breaks, it is integral to include some form of relaxation technique as part of your day. Meditative practices like mindfulness meditation or guided visualization can have profound effects on your ability to manage ADHD and maximize hyperfocus. These techniques not only aid in relaxing your brain but also can enhance your ability to control your attention and reduce impulsivity.

Mindfulness in particular, being a practice of fully focusing on the present moment without judgment, serves dual benefits. It's like a workout for your attention span, increasing your ability to bring your focus back when it wanders. Simultaneously, it relaxes your brain, reducing distractions caused by anxiety or restlessness.

Learning to breathe properly can also do wonders for your focus and well-being. Simple breathing exercises, such as deep diaphragmatic breathing, can lower stress, increase alertness, and enhance cognitive performance. You can include these exercises during your breaks, or set-up separate sessions for them in your daily schedule.

Another beneficial relaxation technique is progressive muscle relaxation. This practice involves tensing and relaxing muscle groups throughout your body, which can help lower overall tension and physical stress. It's a constructive way of using the mind-body connection to reduce the feeling of hyperactivity and to promote physical relaxation which can lead to better focus.

However, it's essential to remember that incorporating breaks and relaxation techniques is not a one-size-fits-all strategy. Take the time to experiment and discover what works best for you. Tailor these strategies in your routine in a way that fits seamlessly and supports your unique style of functioning. Your goal should be to create a balance that will you maintain or re-enter your hyper-focus more comfortably and prevent mental fatigue.

So remember, like a slick car roaring across the highway, your brain, with its unusual wiring, is a marvel that fundamentally benefits from moments of rest. Employ these restorative principles, reap their benefits, and you'll find that mastering your hyper-focus becomes much less a matter of struggle, and much more of an enjoyable and rewarding journey.

Chapter 6: Mastering Hyper-focus - Part 2

Advancing with hyper-focus techniques, I'll be addressing now how hyper-focus ties in to the dreaded practice of multitasking. Blending these two seemingly polar opposites might seem as peculiar as mixing oil and water, but in reality, hyper-focusing can help reign in the chaos swirling in your mind and help achieve multitasking effectively. Observe daily activities; recognize the potential for hyper-focus. Washing dishes, taking a shower, preparing a cup of coffee - any task, mundane or significant, can be done with hyper-focus. It's about layering attention to detail on top of every activity, thereby enhancing the quality of the act and establishing a rhythmic flow to your work. Speaking of work, let's discuss procrastination. Ever-expanding to-do lists are indeed intimidating, and when you're already struggling with staying on a task, they can be downright scary. But here's the kicker: hyper-focus is your secret weapon against procrastination. When you're deeply engrossed in a task, there's no space for thoughts about that cake in the fridge or the latest episode on Netflix. It's like you've entered a tunnel where the only direction to go is forward, towards the completion of your task.

Advanced Hyper-focus techniques

Now that we have a solid grounding in the world of hyper-focus, let's take it up a notch. It's time to delve deeper and uncover some advanced techniques that can guide us to harnessing our hyper-focus. Building upon the principles laid out in our previous chapter, these techniques extend beyond basic hyper-focus management, offering ways to apply and maintain hyper-focus strategically in a range of tasks and situations. We're about to bolster the skill of attention, allowing you to seize your unique capacity for intense focus and make it a productive asset.

First, let's examine the concept of timeboxing. Timeboxing and ADHD might feel like mutually exclusive realms, given our tendency to lose track of time when consumed by hyper-focus. But, when we master the art of timeboxing, we can turn it into a powerful strategy. It involves delimiting a specific time frame to conduct a particular task or activity. With timeboxing, we're applying boundaries to our bouts of hyper-focus, helping to harness this power more effectively.

Next, we step into the realm of mental contrasting. Think of it as envisioning the contrast between your current situation and the goal you want to achieve. This technique fosters motivation, wards off procrastination, and can help you harness your hyper-focus powers. In essence, it makes your aims tangible, pulling them from the abstract into a vivid mental picture that can propel you into action.

Yet another technique to bring to your focal arsenal is the Pomodoro strategy. This method might ring a bell as it has become quite popular in the productivity sphere. The Pomodoro Technique capitalizes on the concept of working with time, not against it. It involves chunking your time into 25-minute sections of intense work (or whatever time limit suits you) followed by a short 5-minute break. Much like timeboxing, this helps manage hyper-focus and prevents burnout.

Mindfulness might seem like a word that's been thrown around a lot these days, but when applied correctly, it holds immense potential for people with ADHD. Cultivating mindfulness allows us to become more aware of our thoughts and actions, aiding us in regaining control over our patterns of hyper-focus. Mindfulness promotes our ability to focus attention on demand and not just when our interest is piqued. By staying present and aware, we're better equipped to steer our hyper-focus into fruitful channels.

Another concept we should talk about is 'mental rehearsal'. Just as an athlete repeatedly visualizes their performance before a big game, mental rehearsal allows you to visualize the task at hand. This not only prepares you for it but can also work to kickstart your hyper-focus. Mental rehearsal can come in quite handy for tasks that might not inherently interest you, by helping create a pathway towards engaging your focus.

Let's now delve into 'active engagement'. What do we mean by this? It's getting physically and psychologically involved with the task at hand. This can mean anything from jotting down notes instead of merely reading, or diving deep into a project instead of sticking to the surface. Active engagement fuels our interest, sparking our hyper-focus to light up even the most mundane task.

The technique of 'switching tasks' can be a game-changer. This doesn't mean multitasking (as we established before, multitasking can be detrimental to focus). Instead, it provides an energy shift by moving from one task to another. This change-up can serve as a mental palate cleanser and can prevent the stagnation of focus. When you find your hyper-focus fading or straying, shifting your attention to a different task can bring it roaring back.

We can't forget 'cueing'. Cueing is a way to set yourself up for success. It involves using a visual or auditory cue—a sticky note, a timer, a reminder app—to prompt an action. These reminders serve to kick your hyper-focus into gear when it is time to start a task or to serve as trigger points to keep you on track throughout the day.

We all know the power of reward. There is significant value in 'rewarding progress', both in motivating us before a task and in maintaining hyper-focus during it. Outline rewards for yourself tied directly to your progress. This reinforcement can keep your attention from straying, maintaining a laser-like focus on the task at hand.

Ultimately, these advanced techniques open up possibilities for gaining command over our hyper-focus. Each method can be shaped to your individual preferences. What matters most is finding the right blend of techniques that resonates with you. Trial and error are essential, as what works marvels for one person might not for another. Be patient with yourself, remain steadfast, and eventually, you'll find the golden key that unlocks your unique hyper-focus capacities.

Remember, mastering hyper-focus is not a sprint, but a marathon. It's a perpetual journey of learning, adjusting, implementing, and refining. But, with these techniques in your toolkit, you're well-equipped to tackle the path ahead. Steer your course confidently, armed with the understanding that your presumed 'flaws' can transform into your most profound strengths if channeled correctly.

Having boosted your hyper-focus skills with these advanced techniques, we will tackle in the next chapter how to apply this knowledge to daily life and tasks. We'll dig deeper into practical strategies and examples to overcome procrastination, taking you a step closer towards tapping into your potential fully. The journey continues!

Hyper-focus and Multitasking might feel like square pegs and round holes when it comes to the concept of ADHD. It's true, there's a common belief that people with ADHD can't multitask efficiently due to how the condition affects the brain. But while it's not completely off the mark, it's not entirely accurate either. Can we, in fact, elegantly juggle multiple tasks simultaneously, wearing the hat of a master juggler? You'd be surprised to know, and astoundingly, yes, we indeed can!

Now, you might be skeptical. That's fair. Often, people think of ADHD as an inability to focus or concentrate on a single task. But here's where we're going to flip the script on its head. ADHD presents an ability called hyper-focus - a state of intense concentration where we can block out almost everything else around us, and that's our ace in the hole. Hyper-focus can be a pretty nifty tool for multitasking when harnessed correctly.

The science behind this isn't as complicated as we might think. Imagine you're a car. Normal focus is your everyday driving mode. You go from point A to B; you're alert but not excessively. Hyper-focus is like putting that car into race mode. Everything fades away except for the road ahead, and you're in control handling multiple factors like speed, direction, and obstacles. Similarly, in our brain, hyper-focus ramps up our attention and concentration levels, allowing us to handle multiple tasks with precision.

That's not to say multitasking on hyper-focus comes naturally. It's kind of like patting your head and rubbing your stomach at the same time - feels weird initially. The trick here is, rather than trying to split your focus, switch between tasks with short bursts of hyper-focus. Rotate your tasks, give each one your undivided attention, and switch when you feel your attention ebbing. It's about recognizing your rhythm, knowing when to push, and when to pull back.

So, yes, you can totally pull off being a multitasking maestro despite ADHD, and even perhaps because of it, with careful planning and a good understanding of your hyper-focus. Will it be messy at first? Probably. Will you drop a ball or two? Maybe. But remember, it's all about practice and patience. Take it slow, take it easy, and before you know it, you'll be juggling tasks like a pro. And remember, every maestro once had to first play the scales.

Using Hyper-focus in Daily Activities is arguably one of the greatest game-changers when learning to be productive with ADHD. Life, in all its unpredictable glory, needs us to juggle many activities for various demands each day—from grocery shopping to important work meetings, daily chores to creative projects. The good news is, your brain is designed to help, particularly when it comes to hyper-focus, the special superpower that comes with the 'ADHD package'.

At its most basic, hyper-focus is the capacity for intense, prolonged concentration on a task, interesting or not, until it's completed. However, it's like walking a tightrope over a yawning chasm of distraction. So, mastering it requires more than just willpower. It's a well-devised strategy, an intentional harnessing of the brain, and a dance with the ADHD waves you're riding.

Imagine hyper-focus as your built-in productivity GPS, guiding you to finish line after finish line. For people with ADHD, entering into the hyper-focus state is as natural as breathing. The trick is directing it. Instead of focusing on fighting distractions or stay on track, why not use that energy to deliberately turn your supercharged focus onto daily tasks? Once you learn how to shift into hyper-focus mode intentionally, you can apply it, ballerina-like, in the pirouettes of daily activities. From deep-cleaning a room to finishing complex work tasks, your ADHD brain can be harnessed for productive use.

Say you're taking on a cleaning project. Traditional strategies may have you drowning in dust bunnies in minutes, distracted by a dozen other tasks. But with hyper-focus, you're in the zone. You may start with reorganizing a bookshelf, move on to dusting, vacuuming, mopping, and before you know it, the entire room is spick and span, leaving you with a sense of accomplishment and a cleaner space. All you need is the right stimuli—a favorite punk rock album, an interesting podcast, or even the ticking clock—and you're set.

In an office or school setting, hyper-focus takes on an artsy grace. You start with a strategic intention—get project X done by lunch—and just like a conductor leading an orchestra, you direct your focus to the task and watch the symphony of productivity unfold in perfect harmony. Grasp the poetry of hyper-focus, and your daily grind can sing with the music of accomplishment. Redirecting your ADHD tendency to hyper-focus from distractions to tasks is like flipping a switch. Work isn't an uphill battle anymore. It's a dance where every step, no matter how routine, contributes to crafting beautiful results.

The Importance of Hyper-focus in Overcoming Procrastination

In a world where distractions are just a click away, it becomes crucial for us to put emphasis on hyper-focus, especially as a strategy to combat procrastination. You see, for individuals with ADHD in their mid-twenties, procrastination is often a formidable adversary. It constantly lurks in the corner, ready to seize any moment of distraction.

But fear not, the key to unlocking an efficient work method that keeps procrastination at bay might just be lying within your very own ADHD.

Remember when we discussed how people with ADHD often find themselves in a state of hyper-focus? This intense concentration can be a game changer when it comes to overcoming procrastination. The secret lies in understanding and leveraging this power to its fullest potential. So let's dive in!

How are hyper-focus and procrastination linked, you might ask. Well, they both revolve around our attention span and, more importantly, what we decide to funnel our attention toward. When we procrastinate, it's usually because we're putting off tasks we perceive as difficult, stressing or less enjoyable. The end result is focusing on something else, usually less productive stuff. Here is where we can use hyper-focus as a tool.

In a nutshell, hyper-focus allows us to sink into a task and block out other distractions. It keeps us firmly seated in the moment, deeply engrossed in whatever we're doing. Can you see how this might be beneficial when we're trying to battle procrastination? Instead of getting lost in endless scrolls on social media, the intense focus demanded by hyper-focus keeps us glued to the task at hand.

That said, it's important to remember that not every task will be inherently interesting enough to engage our hyper-focus. Some stuff will just be boring or tedious. But even then, hyper-focus can come to the rescue. You see, when we can't change the task, we can change our attitude and approach toward it. Giving a task the weight and importance it deserves can often make it worthy of our hyper-focus.

So then, hyper-focus, as beneficial as it sounds, must be sought intentionally. It isn't always an automatic process you can switch on when convenient. Which means you will need to develop strategies to consciously enter this zone.

Firstly, feed your curiosity about the task. Investigate the implications of completing the task or the consequences of ignoring it. Often times, when we enhance our understanding of what it means to carry out a task, our brain finds it interesting enough to stick with it.

Next, dig deep and find an aspect that captures your interest. Even in the most dreary tasks, there's often one point that we can relate to or find intriguing. Identifying and engaging with that point can help coax your brain into hyper-focus mode.

Here's something more pragmatic: consider breaking down bigger tasks into smaller ones. It kinda works like appetizers before the main course, priming the palate or, in our case, priming your focus. When we complete smaller tasks, it creates a sense of achievement and increases the dopamine level in our brains, which then boosts our motivation to continue with the remaining tasks.

Also, bear in mind the right environment matters. A peaceful, distraction-free zone can put us in the right mind space to engage in hyper-focus.

Remember, hyper-focus isn't about turning you into a workaholic. Incorporating breaks, relaxing, and taking care of yourself are equally important. Striving for a balance rather than the extreme ends is what hyper-focus seeks.

In essence, hyper-focus can be like a superpower. When wielded appropriately, it has the potential to turn you into a productivity master, effortlessly juggling tasks that you might have once procrastinated on. Remember that even if you have ADHD, it's not a limitation, but rather, if used correctly, a unique tool in your toolbox on the path of life.

So friends, it's time to dive deep, to immerse completely and partake in the adventure that the hyper-focus state offers. And in this journey, you'll find procrastination falling by the wayside, a fading shadow in the brilliant light of your focus. With the power of hyper-focus, you're not just battling procrastination, but also paving the path for fulfilling productivity.

Chapter 7: Harnessing the Power of Hyper-focus

Continuing from where we left off, it's time to move from theory to practical application. Hyper-focus, with all its raw inherent strength, is a tad like wielding a double-edged sword. It can carve out masterpieces or wreak havoc if left untamed. So, how does one master this power to move from being a procrastinator to a doer? You'll get to read some real-life success stories later on, and they're just a testament to the fact that it can be done! But first, let's discuss maintenance. Maintaining hyper-focus for the long-term, not just during brief stints of inspired action, is something that requires an established routine. There are certain tips and tricks we'll delve into, from mindfulness exercises to time-management techniques, that all contribute to fostering an environment of sustainable efficiency. This isn't just about working hard; it's about working smart. It's about converting those bursts of concentrated energy into a consistent, steady stream. For your hyper-focus isn't a sprinter that needs to exhaust itself in short races; instead, think of it as a marathon runner, strong and steady, ready to go the distance.

From Procrastinator to Doer: Real Life Success Stories

After getting to know the basics and advancements of hyper-focus, you may still have some lingering doubts. Does it truly work? Well, let's dive into some real-life stories of people with ADHD who transformed their lives through hyper-focus techniques.

First, let's meet Brian. Brian, a 24-year-old graphic designer with ADHD, always struggled with deadlines. He was awash in great ideas, formidable talent, and a dynamic creative mind. But his ideas rarely translated into action, and his tasks remained undone. Then he discovered hyper-focus. By amplifying his natural ability to intensely concentrate with ADHD, he was able to harness his mind's full power. Now, he's a successful designer, not despite his ADHD, but because of it.

Consider another example. Claire, aged 28, works in the tech industry, one that is fast-paced and requires a keen focus. While she initially struggled with the workload and deadlines due to her ADHD, Claire embarked on a journey of trial and error with hyper-focus. The outcome? She graduated from being the employee, always behind schedule, to navigating her way to a promotion.

Next up is Melissa, a writer. Sure, she had ideas, stories swirling around in her mind - these were never a problem. The challenge was harnessing these thoughts long enough to pen them down. With the hyper-focus technique, she found a way around it. Melissa now juggles writing columns for multiple publications, and even has a few published novels under her belt, all thanks to hyper-focus.

David's tale is equally inspiring. As a college student with ADHD, he always had a tough time focusing on his studies. By leveraging hyper-focus, he discovered a way to channel his scattered energy into productive focus. A big project or essay due wasn't a crisis to be averted anymore, but a challenge to conquer. David's grades improved dramatically.

Cassie, a project manager, was always bouncing from one incomplete project to the other due to her inability to stay focused. This resulted in delayed deadlines, causing dissatisfaction among her team members. But when she channeled hyper-focus, it was like everything fell into place. Projects were completed on time, and her productivity soared, earning her due recognition and respect from her team.

Even as a teenager, Steve had big dreams of becoming an entrepreneur. But his ADHD was a hurdle he didn't know how to overcome until he discovered hyper-focus. He launched his start-up, and lo and behold, he emerged as a successful entrepreneur, showing that the future is unwritten and can indeed be molded with determination and the right techniques.

Meg is a busy mom who has ADHD, which can make it tough to manage everyday tasks and her children's schedules. However, everything started falling into place once she understood and applied hyper-focus techniques. Now, she breezes through the tasks and maintains a lovely balance between her life and children's schedules. Meg is living proof that hyper-focus isn't confined to work or studies alone but can be applied meaningfully in everyday life chores as well.

Aaron, an architect, had a remarkable vision but struggled with the execution, unable to continue focus for minutes at a time. By incorporating hyper-focus, he was able to marshal his scattered attention into crafting masterful plans to fruition. Now he is a respected figure in his field.

Lastly, we have Sam who, despite ADHD, was always curious and loved to learn. But the traditional educational system clashed with his learning style, causing anxiety and self-doubt. Once he learned about hyper-focus, his academic fortunes transformed. Sam's story stands testament that ADHD doesn't have to hold back a curious and keen mind from achieving greatness.

Each of these individuals found unique ways to leverage hyper-focus techniques despite their ADHD. You too can achieve your personal and professional goals, just like them. It may not happen overnight, but with persistence and the right techniques, your transformation from procrastinator to doer is completely possible.

The roadblocks of ADHD are not insurmountable; they can be turned into stepping stones with the right set of skills. And hyper-focus is a powerful tool that can help you do just that. So, believe in your ability to change and grow, because the power to become a 'doer' lies within you.

No story highlighted here was a promise of an easy journey or a magical transformation. They each faced setbacks, had their flusters, and tangled with their doubts. But ultimately, they all persevered. They understood their unique mindsets and learned to work with, not against their ADHD, using hyper-focus to their advantage.

These stories help debunk the myth that having ADHD is a liability. Instead, they demonstrate that it can be a unique strength when harnessed correctly. As someone with ADHD, you can not only overcome challenges and succeed, but you can also possess a distinct vantage point that sets you apart.

With the right tools, your naturally creative, energetic and resilient ADHD mind can become a powerful conduit for achievement. Brian, Claire, Melissa, David, Cassie, Steve, Meg, Aaron, and Sam understood this, and so can you. Remember how they went from procrastinator to doer, and know that the same transformation is certainly within your reach.

Maintaining Hyper-focus Long-Term in Daily Life

Alright! Now that we've discovered hyper-focus as an ADHD superpower and understood how to harness it, the challenge is maintaining it long-term. Hyper-focus presents a unique opportunity for individuals with ADHD to shine, but to truly tap into the benefits, you require consistent practice. It's akin to a muscle that needs to be flexed over time to remain strong.

How do we maintain hyper-focus for longer periods without burning out or giving in to distractions? Here are some scientifically based, proven techniques and strategies that you can incorporate into your daily life.

First, take care of your physical health. This might seem like an unrelated factor, but studies have shown that our ability to focus and maintain attention is directly impacted by our physical wellbeing. This means eating well, getting enough exercise, and getting plenty of sleep. A healthy body fuels a healthy mind. So, make sure to prioritize a balanced diet, regular exercise, and at least 7-9 hours of sleep every night.

Secondly, try creating a "hyper-focus routine". This is a set sequence of activities or tasks that you do regularly to enter your hyper-focus state. A routine can be especially helpful because it reduces the amount of mental effort you need to spend on starting a task. And don't forget to change this routine or mix it up whenever you feel like it's starting to become stale or less effective. Remember, novelty can be a potent stimulant for the ADHD brain.

Next, learning to manage distractions is critical. With ADHD, you might find that your attention shifts quickly from one thing to another. In such cases, identifying potential sources of distractions and finding effective ways to limit them optimizes your time in the hyper-focus zone. This could mean turning off unnecessary notifications on your phone, creating an uncluttered workspace, or even using noise-canceling headphones to avoid auditory distractions.

The Pomodoro Technique is another practical strategy for maintaining focus. This involves breaking your work into 25-minute intervals (or "pomodoros") followed by a 5-minute break. Once you complete four pomodoros, take a longer break of about 15-30 minutes. This method can be particularly effective for those with ADHD as it provides a balance between intense focus and periods of rest. Plus, the anticipation of a scheduled break can make the focus period seem more manageable.

Another aspect is to embrace a mindfulness practice. Often, maintaining focus is challenging because of the rush of thoughts in your head. Mindfulness, which can be practiced through activities like meditation, can help clear your mind, making it easier to maintain focus.

Visual reminders and tools are huge assists in maintaining focus. Bullet journals, for instance, provide a physical and visual representation of your tasks and goals. They allow you to clearly see what needs to be done and provide a satisfying way to track your progress.

Avoid task stacking, where you plan to do several things simultaneously. For persons with ADHD, this can lead to a scattered focus, reduced productivity, and increased mental fatigue. Instead, prioritize your tasks and focus on completing one before moving on to the next.

Strategically manage your energy levels, not just your time. As an individual with ADHD, you might notice that your focus and energy levels fluctuate throughout the day. By recognizing your natural rhythms, you can schedule your most demanding tasks during your peak energy times and less-demanding tasks during your low-energy periods.

Finally, being patient with yourself and celebrating milestones is critical. There will be days when your focus is less than optimal, and that's okay. Hyperfocusing is a skill, and like all skills, it takes time to master. During this journey, it's important to celebrate your progress, no matter how small or insignificant it may seem.

Maintaining hyper-focus long-term in daily life may seem challenging initially, but the rewards are worth it. By incorporating these strategies into your routine, in due time, you could complete tasks more efficiently, find deeper enjoyment in activities you love, and gain a sense of accomplishment.

Remember, ADHD isn't a barrier to success. In fact, with the right tools, it can even be a unique advantage. So, welcome the ebbs and flows of your attention and use them to your advantage to power up your productivity. Cheers to your journey towards mastering hyper-focus!

Other Tips and Tricks to Increase Hyper-focus

The beauty of hyper-focus is in its power to release productivity potential like nothing else. But hyper-focus isn't necessarily a state you just slip into. It requires nurturing, practice, and patience to cultivate. Here are some additional tips and tricks that could help increase your hyper-focus.

First, pay attention to your personal rhythms. You know yourself better than anyone else. If you've always been a morning person, getting up early may be the best time for you to achieve your hyper-focus. On the opposite, if you feel more energized in the later parts of the day, consider scheduling your most important tasks in the afternoon or evening. Learn to work with your internal clock, not against it.

Let's talk about meditation. Meditation can be an incredible tool to cultivate awareness, focus, and calm. Even a few minutes spent quieting your mind can lead to increased ability to hyper-focus. Remember, you don't need to become a Zen master to reap the benefits of this practice. Even five minutes a day can make a significant difference over time.

Try using visualization as a technique. This not only applies to your tasks but also your desired results. Imagine yourself ticking off your to-dos without any hurdles. Visualize the successful completion of the task. This mental imagery will stimulate your motivation and concentration.

Implement a reward system. Give yourself a treat after successfully completing a challenging task. This doesn't always have to be a physical reward, sometimes just the action of ticking off a task can provide a dopamine hit – that feel-good chemical in your brain. The anticipation of a reward can spur you to maintain your focus.

Leverage the power of music. Everyone's different; some people work best in complete silence while some prefer having some background noise. If you're in the latter category, consider opting for instrumental music. The absence of lyrics can prevent cognitive overload and promote a sense of serenity, aiding in hyper-focus.

Try to limit distractions and multi-tasking. These are two of the biggest killers of focus. Make sure your environment is set up to keep distractions minimized. And even though some of us fancy ourselves as adept multi-taskers, the truth is the human brain is wired to tackle one thing at a time. You'll achieve better results focusing on one task at a breeze.

Find an accountability buddy. This could be a friend, family member, or colleague, who can hold you accountable to your goals. Sharing your objectives with someone else can be surprisingly effective for maintaining your focus and motivation.

Consider incorporating exercise into your daily routine. Just as it's important to exercise your mind, exercising your body can lead to increased mental sharpness, attentiveness and even improve your mood. It doesn't have to be an intensive workout, even a walk around the block can do wonders.

Get enough sleep. It might seem like a no-brainer, but numerous studies have shown that a lack of good quality sleep can significantly impair your concentration levels. Try to stick to a consistent sleep schedule and ensure your bedroom is a conducive environment for sleep.

Avoid skipping meals. Nutritious food is brain-fuel, keep it in top gear by maintaining a balanced diet. Also staying well hydrated throughout the day aids in maintaining focus.

Appreciate your achievements, no matter how big or small. Pat yourself on the back for completing a tough assignment or simply just maintaining focus for longer than usual. It's a journey, after all, so why not celebrate along the way?

Keep a journal to reflect on your progress. Write down what's working, what isn't, and how you're feeling. This will not only help you know yourself better but will also highlight any patterns or potential obstacles.

Lastly, remember the importance of perseverance. Learning to hyper-focus takes time and practice, and that's perfectly okay. There will be bumps along the way, but don't let those discourage you. Keep the end goal in mind, and keep going.

These additional tips and tricks complement the ones you've learned so far. Implement them, play around with them, and see what works best for you. Remember, the aim is to put in place practical measures that encourage and nurture your ability to hyper-focus.

Now, you have a robust tool chest filled with strategies to cultivate hyper-focus. Remember, hyper-focus isn't an all or nothing deal, and it's certainly not a magic pill. It's more of a progression, a journey of learning to tune into your strengths, work with your rhythms, and channel your concentration to work for you. Your journey to mastering hyper-focus may not be quick and trouble-free, but it will most certainly be rewarding.

Moving Beyond Procrastination

Now that we've covered the ins and outs of hyper-focus, let's shift our focus to shaking off the chains of procrastination. You've probably found that when you're interested in a task, you can dive in with full focus, whether it's a hobby or a fascinating work assignment. But when it's something tedious or uninteresting, that's when the procrastination bug really bites. So, how do we take that powerful focusing tool that's hardwired into our ADHD brains and apply it to tasks we'd rather avoid? Let's start by setting some achievable goals and breaking them down into bite-sized pieces. This may sound simple, but it's incredibly important. And we're not just talking about big, life-altering goals, but everyday tasks as well. The key is to break down these tasks into manageable parts, making it less overwhelming. Next, we're going to explore some time-tested cognitive strategies and techniques designed to alter negative thought patterns, effectively retraining your brain so that it becomes more second nature to get to work, rather than defer it. Besides, we're not neglecting the fact that a healthy mind rests in a healthy body. Indeed, the relationship between ADHD, focus and our diet and physical wellbeing cannot be overstated. So, we will take a look into the critical role of nutrition and exercise. Remember, the aim here is not only to move beyond procrastination, but also shape sustainable, healthy habits that create a more productive and focused you.

Setting Goals and Breaking them Down

You've already mastered the art of hyper-focus using the previously outlined techniques. Still feeling a little overwhelmed? Don't worry, that's a perfectly normal response to major self-improvement. Now, let's talk about setting ambitious goals and breaking them down into manageable tasks. Doing this takes into account both our ADHD quirks and our ability to hyper-focus.

First off, let's be clear about what a goal is. You should envision it as your finish line—the point you're striving to reach. It's a vision of something you deeply desire to accomplish. But how do we tackle goals effectively, especially when ADHD can all too often derail our best intentions?

A goal has to be specific. Let's not just say "I want to get fit", instead, specify it like "I want to be able to run five miles without taking a break in two months." With ADHD, the more concrete our goals, the better.

The goal also has to be measurable. What does "getting fit" look like? Instead, decide on a set distance or time you want to run without getting winded. Maybe that's a five-mile run, or a 30-minute continuous jog, or even executing a complete yoga routine.

Furthermore, your goal should be achievable. It's essential to be ambitious, but your goals should still be within the realms of possibility. If you've barely run more than half a mile before, trying to master a marathon within a month might be setting the bar too high.

Importantly, for goals to be effective, they need to be relevant. Choose something that makes a genuine difference to your life, something that you passionately want to achieve. If it's important, you'll work harder for it.

Finally, your goal needs to be time-bound, having a clear deadline. That's how we can use our hyper-focus superpower to our advantage. With an end date in sight, we can channel our intensity towards achieving our goals effectively.

Getting grip on our goals can be difficult sometimes but remember, they can always be adjusted. You may find that you need more time to accomplish your goal, or that the goal itself needs refining. And that's perfectly okay. Flexibility is a sign of strength, not weakness.

Breaking our goals down into chunks or steps is another crucial technique. Start by identifying the big steps that need to be taken to reach your goal. For example, if you're trying to run five miles non-stop in two months, some steps might include establishing a regular training schedule, improving your diet to boost energy levels, and investing in good running shoes.

From the bigger steps, break actions down further into tasks or to-do's that can be completed in a day. To stick with our running example, maybe on Day 1 you research and buy the best running shoes for you. On Day 2, you run for ten minutes, and so on. It's these mini-achievements that accumulate into larger wins.

Daily tasks convert into weeks, weeks become months and, before you know it, you're at your goal. And, while you've hustled for every step, it won't have felt like a slog because you were effectively leveraging the benefits of your ADHD, like hyper-focus.

Consider using a tool or method to track your progress. It could be as simple as a journal or a checklist, or a more structured approach like a project management tool. Seeing your progress visualized can often bring that much-needed motivation to keep pushing forward.

As much as this chapter is about setting goals and breaking them down, perhaps the most critical takeaway from it should be this: Be kind to yourself. Success isn't linear, and everybody stumbles. What sets the achievers apart is they get back up and keep working towards their goal.

After all, when you set substantial goals and break them down, you're not only creating a path to victory; you're also harnessing the power of ADHD. This way, you tackle life on your terms, using your quirks and qualities to your advantage, not as a hindrance. This is your journey, and ADHD is your superpower. Use it wisely.

Retraining Your Brain

After adjusting your environment, setting goals, and recognizing the potential of hyper-focus, it's time to discuss an equally important aspect: retraining your brain. Understanding the need to alter thinking patterns is key to productivity, especially if you're managing ADHD. We'll elucidate the neuroplasticity principle and how to utilize it to your advantage. Let's dive right in!

Our brains are constantly changing. This ability is known as neuroplasticity. The brain adapts to new experiences, from learning language, solving math problems, to memorizing song lyrics. Similarly, it's feasible to recondition your brain to work optimally even with ADHD.

First things first, belief systems are powerful. In fact, it's been scientifically proven that our mental state, as shaped by our beliefs, can directly impact our productivity and overall life satisfaction. If you're constantly convinced that ADHD sets limitations, those limiting thoughts can indeed become a self-fulfilling prophecy. To break free, you need to reframe your beliefs and see ADHD not as a setback, but as a unique capability.

This is where the trick of cognitive reframing comes in. Cognitive reframing is a psychological technique involving the identification and then dispute of irrational or maladaptive thoughts. It's about altering your perspective on a situation or a condition. Instead of viewing your ADHD as a barrier, reframe it as a set of unique characteristics that make you who you are.

Followed by reframing, mindful thinking is crucial. Being mindful can lead to enhanced focus and lower stress levels, both of which can aid in managing ADHD symptoms. By being consciously aware of your mental processes, you're more capable of spotting distractions and refocusing your attention when it wanders off.

Practicing mindful meditation can be a great start for promoting awareness and control over your attention. Mindfulness training can include simple breathing exercises or meditations, where you focus on your breathing and let thoughts come and go without judgment. Not only can it help you manage your ADHD, but it can also reduce stress and improve your overall mood.

Visualization is another tool to retrain your brain. Picture yourself accomplishing tasks with ease, staying focused, and achieving your goals. The more frequently you can visualize these positive outcomes, the easier it will be to bring them into reality.

One more thing that deserves attention is self-talk. The language you use when thinking about yourself or your abilities can greatly influence your capability to handle tasks. Choosing to use positive and empowering language is a simple yet powerful way to keep your motivation high and your aim sharp.

Besides mental exercises, physical activities also play an important role in retraining your brain. Regular physical activity stimulates the production of endorphins, which are known to help concentration and improve mood. Activities that require body and mind coordination, like yoga or martial arts, can be particularly beneficial.

Also important to mention is the role diet plays in your cognitive function. Consuming nutrient-dense food can lead to better mind-body balance. Limit the intake of processed foods and consume a balanced diet high in fruits, vegetables, lean proteins, and whole grains. It's not a magic remedy, but a healthy diet can absolutely help your brain function more effectively.

We can't underscore enough the importance of a proper sleep routine. Lack of adequate sleep can worsen ADHD symptoms. Therefore, establishing a regular sleep schedule and creating an environment conducive to good sleep are some of the best things you can do for your brain health and productivity.

And last, regular check-ins with yourself are a practical way to stay accountable. Reflect on how well you are able to manage distractions, stick to tasks, and whether your mind wanders less or more. These self-reflections can help you adjust your approach while also celebrating your progress.

Yes, retraining your brain with ADHD can seem daunting initially. But remember, every journey begins with one small step. Embrace your uniqueness, practice, and be patient with yourself. The more you exercise these strategies, the more second-nature they will become. And soon enough, you'll see your productivity soaring high!

Nurturing your Mind: Importance of Nutrition and Exercise

With the right tools in your hands, you've been making significant strides towards mastering hyper-focus and overcoming procrastination. But harnessing the power of ADHD isn't just about training the mind. Wellness in all aspects of life is key, which brings us to the next aspect of embracing ADHD—in this chapter, the focus will be on nutrition and exercise. Both are essential to provide the stamina, energy, and mental acuity needed to utilize your hyper-focus effectively.

First up is nutrition; the food we fuel our bodies with has a significant impact on how our brains function. A healthy, balanced diet can support your cognitive functions, boost your focus, increase your mood stability, and, of course, give you the energy required to face your day head-on.

If you're asking yourself the question, what should I eat? The answer is simple, opt for whole, unprocessed foods. Get in plenty of colorful fruits and vegetables, lean proteins like chicken and fish, and good, healthy fats from things like avocados, whole eggs, nuts and seeds, and olive oil. Also, ensure you eat enough complex carbs, like brown rice or quinoa, to sustain energy levels throughout the day.

Just as important is what you shouldn't eat. Avoid processed, sugary foods—they can mess with your glucose levels and lead to energy crashes that make concentration and focus all the more difficult. It's not about deprivation, it's about balance. Allow yourself the occasional treat, but make nourishing your body a priority.

Another important factor often overlooked is hydration. Our brains need water to function optimally, so getting into the habit of drinking enough throughout the day can be an effective way to sharpen focus and reduce symptoms of ADHD.

Alright, now that we've covered the nutrition part, let's delve into the exercise element. Exercise and physical activity serve multiple purposes. In one way, they're just good for the body, right? They help maintain a healthy weight, boost heart health, increase energy levels, and promote good sleep. But did you know that exercise also has massive brain benefits? In fact, it's one of the most powerful tools we can use to improve our mental health.

Regular exercise has proven to be beneficial for people with ADHD because it can reduce symptoms, improve concentration and memory, and enhance mood and overall mental well-being. Isn't it incredible that working up a sweat can do so much good for your brain?

And the good news is, any sort of movement counts! Find something that you enjoy doing, whether that's weightlifting, running, dancing, or yoga. The key is to make it a consistent practice—aim for at least 30 minutes of moderate-intensity exercise most days a week. Mix it up to keep things interesting, repeat what feels good, and remember, it's about progress, not perfection.

Moving the body regularly also decreases excess energy and restlessness, which can interfere with focus. It helps you sleep better, critical for brain function and peak performance. In both indirect and direct ways, exercise can contribute to your ability to use your hyper-focus to accomplish your goals.

In the same breath, exercise doesn't mean pushing yourself to the point of exhaustion. Make sure to also incorporate some calming, slow-paced activities, like yoga or tai chi. Relaxation and muscle-strengthening activities like these can lower stress and improve emotional regulation, supporting a more focused mind.

Well, there you have it. Nutrition and exercise, when paired with the mental strategies we've already discussed, form an unbeatable trio. Embrace these as critical components of your ADHD survival toolkit. Nurture your body, nurture your mind, and watch as these practices complement one another, reinforcing your greatest asset—your ADHD-powered mental agility.

Remember that this isn't about achieving perfection. It's about being more nurturing to your mind and body. While ADHD can make this self-care a little bit more challenging, you have all the resources you need to step up and succeed. Trust in your ability to improve, and let the power of steady, healthy habits fuel your journey.

Taking Control of Your Life

As we move ahead that the first step to taking control of your life and leveraging your ADHD to work in your favor, the power lies within implementing the strategies. Implementation can be intimidating—it's like staring at a blank canvas, overwhelmed with choice. However, taking one small step at a time can prove worthwhile. Each tool, method, or ideology, from understanding your ADHD to using hyper-focus, from breaking down goals and retraining your brain, it all boils down to the hunger in you to adopt them every day, over and over. Acknowledging the thought of change, embracing it—one fine day, you look back to see how far you've traveled from that initial change, leading to transforming your life. *It's real – you're not just faking it till you make it, you're living it!* Life truly opens up when you stand unafraid, harnessing your unique attributes, sprinkling your journey with the philosophy of resilience.

Implementing the Strategies

Now that you are well immersed in the robust world of understanding ADHD, hyper-focus, and their surprising potential, it's high time to tackle the implementation phase. We are transitioning from theory to action, from thinking to doing. The strategies we will delve into here will empower you to actively use your ADHD and hyper-focus as incredible tools in your daily life. Let's get started!

Firstly, consider the environment around you. A calm, clean, and organized environment holds the key to successfully implementing hyper-focus techniques. You are nurturing your brain, and this should reflect in your physical surroundings too. Transform your workspace or any area where you plan to implement your hyper-focus strategy into the most conducive environment for productivity. Embrace simplicity and decluttering; remember, less really can be more.

Next, to harness the power of ADHD, remember that routine is pivotal. If you wish to orient yourself towards a task, having a routine can serve as a brilliant anchor. A step-by-step structure takes less energy to follow and calms your ADHD mind by lessening the number of decisions you must make each day. So, devise, solidify, and follow a routine—a powerful daily playbook to kickstart your productivity.

Then, work around the ADHD trait of being interested in many things at once, which in essence, fuels procrastination. Employ what we may term as the 'interest-based approach'. Attend to tasks when - and only when - they pique your interest intensely. This is a nifty way of tricking your brain into hyperfocus mode and deferring tasks that may not be as captivating until they naturally seize your interest.

Also, note the powerful tool that is time management. With ADHD, your perception of time might be skewed. Combat this by using time management techniques - and this is where tools like timers and alarms will noticeably help. Set a timer for each task you set out to complete. This not only provides a start and end point but also a sense of urgency, encouraging your brain into a state of intense focus.

Alongside time management, try 'brain-dumping' where you jot down every task that you need to accomplish. This clears your mind off the clutter and allows you to focus on one task at a time. Your sticky notes and whiteboards are about to become your trusty sidekicks.

It's also of prime importance to prioritize self-care. This isn't an optional extra; it's a pivotal component. Exercise regularly, maintain a balanced diet, indulge in hobbies and activities that bring you joy. When you take care of your physical well-being, it amplifies your ability to function mentally. Homing your state of hyper-focus becomes easier when your body is in sync with your mental efforts.

Another strategic approach is to get comfortable with discomfort. It's a part of life. Procrastination is often an avoidance technique to dodge discomfort. However, the real growth happens outside of our comfort zones. So as intimidating as it may sound, tackle the things that make you uncomfortable head-on.

Now, don't forget the role of breaks. Your mind needs to rest to perform its best. Ensure you are taking regular intervallic breaks during your hyper-focus sessions. It's not about endurance; it's about balanced efficiency. Remember, it's a marathon, not a sprint.

Also, cultivate the practice of mindfulness. It might sound clichéd, but cultivating mindfulness can significantly help manage ADHD symptoms. It doesn't have to be elaborate; just sitting quietly, focusing on your breath for a few minutes each day can help train your brain to stay focused.

Alongside, cultivate a positive perspective towards ADHD. This is not a flaw or a disorder, but a unique wiring of the brain that can, with the right management techniques, become a source of great strength. A shift in the way you perceive your ADHD can significantly impact how you manage it.

Finally, be patient throughout this journey of implementing strategies. Change often doesn't happen overnight, but trust the process and persevere. You might make mistakes or fall off your routine, but remember, it's about progress, not perfection. This journey is less about fighting against ADHD and more about learning to dance in harmony with it.

Remember, it's your unique journey. Not all of these strategies may work for you, or may even resonate with you. That's perfectly fine. Try out, mix and match, diverge, converge. Make these strategies not just a part of your ADHD journey but also your individual personality. Tailor them to fit you, not the other way round.

Continual trial and error are the keys to unlocking the potent potential of your hyper-focus and ADHD. Remember, knowledge is only as helpful as its application. So, now that we have discussed implementing strategies, it's your turn to step up to the plate and immerse yourself in the vivacity of your ADHD journey!

The next section will help further solidify this journey as we look ahead, brimming with positive anticipation, toward the wonderful possibilities that lie in managing ADHD successfully and nurturing hyper-focus.

A Look Ahead

So, there you have it. ADHD, once viewed as a set back, is now turned into a secret weapon for productivity. You're no longer trapped by uncontrollable procrastination but alternatively, equipped with the power of hyper-focus. Embrace the beauty in your brain's pattern of sprinting, pausing, and restarting. Remember, ADHD doesn't have to limit our life's purpose - it can, in fact, define it. It amplifies the process of hyper-focus, turning a traditional weakness into a stunning strength. Going forward, the trick is in knowing how to get into the zone, and just as critical, when to step back and recharge. Implementing routines, nutrition, and mindfulness can help nurture this process. By mastering and maintaining hyper-focus, you are effectively dialing down on procrastination. Your ADHD brain is not a battleground, but rather a well of untapped potential. Here's to a future of outstanding productivity, my friends. So forge ahead, play this symphony of an energetic, creative, and hyper-focused life.

Conclusion: Embracing ADHD as a Strength

If you've made it this far, you've already accomplished something tremendous. You've acknowledged not just the challenges of ADHD, but its potential as a catalyst for productivity and creativity. You've learned about hyper-focus, how to harness it and how to maximize the advantage it can render for you. Embracing ADHD as a strength is taking the first step toward a brighter, more successful future.

We've done a lot of talking about how ADHD can be used to your advantage, but it's now it's time to put these concepts into practice. The method won't be perfect. Sometimes you might find it tough to tap into your hyper-focus. Other days, procrastination might appear to have the upper hand. What matters is your determination and commitment to keep trying and optimizing your approach.

Remember, too, that everyone's experience with ADHD is unique. So, your path to using ADHD to your advantage will also be exclusive to you. Be patient with yourself along this path, take one step at a time, rejoice in every small victory, and always remind yourself of your progress. But importantly, surround yourself with positivity and acceptance, and keep refining your approach based on what works for you.

Especially when it comes to overcoming procrastination and honing your hyper-focus, it's not going to be a rapid transformation. It takes persistence and patience. It takes understanding yourself better, figuring out what works for you and what doesn't. It requires you to step out of your comfort zone and try new techniques or strategies. But keep going, because the rewards are worth it.

One pivotal aspect of embracing ADHD as a strength is the gift of hyper-focus. It is an extraordinary tool that allows you to dive deep into any task and achieve an unparalleled level of concentration. It enables you to get into 'the zone,' where productivity and creativity flow seamlessly. With learned control and discipline, hyper-focus can be an incredible weapon for productivity, far surpassing what 'normal' focus can achieve.

Still, harnessing hyper-focus isn't just about productivity or efficiency. It's also about empowering you to pursue your passions, engage in activities that you genuinely enjoy, and unlock your potential. Hyper-focus can allow you to thrive in areas where you once struggled, transforming perceived weaknesses into undeniable strengths.

Just remember, your ADHD does not define you, nor should it limit you. Acceptance is crucial because that's when you replace self-judgment with self-compassion. With this newfound acceptance, you can start to redefine your relationship with your ADHD, recognizing it not as a constant bother but as a part of your unique make-up.

Your journey with ADHD is an ongoing one. There'll be good days and bad days, strides of progress, and occasional setbacks. However, it's important not to lose sight of how far you've come and the personal growth you've experienced along the journey.

Keeping an open mind, tapping into your strengths, and fostering resilience will help you on your path to overcoming the challenges you may face. Remember to apply these tips and techniques consistently for long-lasting effects.

Beyond just dealing with procrastination and leveraging hyper-focus, we discussed other aspects of living with ADHD. We considered how a healthy lifestyle and optimal brain nutrition play an essential role in managing ADHD symptoms. Incorporating exercise, maintaining a balanced diet, getting enough sleep, and taking the necessary steps to look after your mental health can significantly contribute towards managing ADHD effectively, so don't ignore these fundamentals.

Embrace ADHD as a strength, not a hindrance. Use it as fuel to drive you forward to achieving your goals, not a blockade that holds you back. Consider it a unique aspect of your identity, not a challenge or setback. Like a superhero's 'special power,' embrace your ADHD and utilize it to your advantage.

Don't forget that it's essential to keep learning, adapting, and growing. Keep the conversation going, both with yourself and others. Encourage open communications about ADHD, its challenges, and its strengths. Foster a supportive network around you, whether it's friends, family, or professionals, who can provide the right support and understanding.

In conclusion, having ADHD is like having a tool in your toolbox that not everyone has. When managed correctly, it can become a valuable asset. It's a unique part of who you are, and you should feel proud to possess such a distinctive strength.

May you always remember to embrace your ADHD as a strength and potential superpower. Here's to your continued growth, success, and brilliance.

Appendix A: Further Reading on ADHD and Hyper-focus

As we take a breather after delving into in-depth exploration, discussions, and strategies regarding ADHD and hyper-focus, it's obvious we've just scratched the surface. There's a whole world of information, studies, theories and philosophies out there waiting for you to dive in deeper. If you're hungry for more, or simply need different perspectives to truly understand and process the topics, here's a brief list of recommended further reading.

For ADHD:

1. *Driven to Distraction: Recognizing and Coping with Attention Deficit Disorder* by Edward M. Hallowell and John J. RateyThis classic self-help book takes a comprehensive look at ADHD, sifting through various symptoms and potential coping mechanisms. It's a great starting point for anyone wanting to understand the fundamentals of ADHD.

2. *ADHD 2.0: New Science and Essential Strategies for Thriving with Distraction—from Childhood through Adulthood* by Edward M. Hallowell and John J. RateyFrom the authors of *Driven to Distraction*, this book provides an updated guide for people with ADHD. It includes discussions on new tools and strategies that incorporate the latest science and technologies.

For Hyper-focus:

1. *Hyperfocus: How to Be More Productive in a World of Distraction* by Chris BaileyThis book goes beyond the realm of ADHD, exploring how anyone can tap into and harness the power of hyper-focus. It's perfect if you're looking to channel your focus and enhance productivity.

2. *The Power of Full Engagement: Managing Energy, Not Time, Is the Key to High Performance and Personal Renewal* by Jim Loehr and Tony SchwartzThis book gives you a fresh perspective, expressing the importance of managing your energy, not just time. Its principles can be adapted to nurture your ability to hyper-focus.

For both ADHD and Hyper-focus:

1. *Scattered Minds: The Origins and Healing of Attention Deficit Disorder* by Gabor MatéMaté presents an interesting perspective that interweaves ADHD and hyper-focus. He provides insights on the origin of ADHD and suggests healing techniques, making this a great read for holistic understanding and improvement.

2. *ADHD and the Focused Mind: A Guide to Giving Your ADHD Child Focus, Discipline, &a Self-Confidence* by Sarah Cheyette, Ben Cheyette, and Peter JohnsonWhile primarily for parents dealing with children with ADHD, this book provides practical strategies to cultivate focus, discipline, and confidence. Its techniques and insights can be adapted and applied to adults with ADHD focusing on hyper-focus.

It's worth exploring these resources to deepen your insights into ADHD and hyper-focus. Remember, every person's journey with these is unique. So, read extensively, experiment with strategies, grab what works for you and discard the rest. Most importantly, go easy on yourself and celebrate your small victories because the road to productivity is paved with patience and constant learning.

Isabelle Palmer

www.ingramcontent.com/pod-product-compliance
Lightning Source LLC
Chambersburg PA
CBHW030353290526
45785CB00004B/1734